I0060057

DIRECT MAIL IS NOT DEAD

*

Grow Your Business With Targeted Direct Mail

Eugene Montanez

Eugene@DirectMailIsNotDead.com
www.DirectMailIsNotDead.com

Anoroc Publishing
P.O. Box 1208
Corona, CA 92878

ISBN: 978-0615946290
LCCN: 21011987

Contents

Eugene Montanez has an extensive background in business, marketing, online services and direct mail, since beginning his business while in high school. Starting in his mother's garage, Eugene has grown his printing business, with his wife Paula, into a modern, digital, printing and marketing firm.

In addition to helping many types of businesses grow with unique marketing ideas, Eugene has also owned other companies, such as JamCaps, an international toy producer, and USA Coaters, an importer of printing machinery from China.

In Eugene's spare time he has served on the City of Corona Planning Commission for 8 years before being elected to the City Council and serving 2 terms as Mayor of Corona, a city in California with a population of 155,000. In his city role, Eugene has also been active in attracting and retaining numerous nationally recognized companies to Corona.

Some of the FREE bonuses available on page 123.

"In business you've got to adapt, change or die; whether you're on Wall Street or Main Street, everyone's goal is to increase the zeros on their bottom line."

—Jeff Hayzlett,

Host of "C-Suite with Jeffrey Hayzlett" on Bloomberg TV

Dedication

This book is dedicated to the people in my life that have shaped my drive and spirit.

First, my wife Paula, who has been my friend, partner and confidant over 37 years. Paula has never wavered in her support, regardless how crazy the idea is!

My constant inspiration has been my late grandfather, Ramon Montanez, who with my grandmother Maria operated a small neighborhood grocery store in front of their home in Los Angeles while he invented new X-ray techniques at LA General Hospital.

My mother Ernestine provided the business sense to know you had to make a profit if you were in business!

My father Bob (Zuma) has been a rocket scientist that helped propel men to the moon, with a sliderule. His career inspired my love of technology.

Last, but not least, Bobby, Angela & Royce Parker Montanez. The next generations are what we all get up every morning for. No pressure, but they are responsible for the future.

Whenever a book gets published you have to ask yourself if it really adds something new to what you already know. This one does. It shows you first-hand, in very practical terms how you can grow your business exponentially and antimimeticisomorphically.

Antimimeticisomorphism simply means doing out-of-the-ordinary things that create extra-ordinary results with the least amount of effort and lowest cost. In common vernacular it's the opposite of 'monkey see, monkey do'. If you do what everyone else does, which means you will get the same results they get and by definition those results are, average. You don't read a book to get average results. You read a book to get an edge, an advantage. This one won't disappoint.

Direct Mail Is Not Dead! reveals step-by-step how to turns the tables upside down by claiming in its title that direct mail is not dead! By so doing, the results you will obtain will be extra-ordinary. This is a counter-intuitive claim validated with substantial proof, including numerous case studies and examples.

Of course if all you do is read the book, your bottom line won't change very much. However, if you read the book proactively and challenge yourself to mirror, adjust, adapt and refine the campaigns and strategies revealed, the sky's the limit.

If you're wondering if you should read this book, consider the sobering failure statistics for businesses. Four out of five businesses fail within five years. Half of the remainder don't make it past the next five... Eugene has been in business for over 40 years!

That means he's in the top 1% of all businesses in America – the survivor, the success story. That's one of the reasons you should read the book. But if this book was just another autobiographical success story, I wouldn't be recommending it.

Let's face it, time is at a premium. You want quick, effective strategies to grow your business. This book reveals how you can get the best 'bang for your buck' by counteracting the fads and trends and doing things that produce real results. Results you can measure. Results that are profitable. Results that can be repeated. Results that can be tailored to your business and your budget.

In this day and age of electronic communications, *Direct Mail Is Not Dead!* Far from it. When combined with other media, direct mail remains one of the most potent prospecting tools available. When mastered, it can virtually eliminate all cold-calling and other time-consuming and costly sales and marketing alternatives.

As you read the following pages, you will discover the most powerful aspect of direct mail marketing – its stealth characteristics. The direct mail strategies proposed usually remain hidden from your competitors so they will never know what you're up, to giving you a decisive and defensible competitive advantage that future-proofs your business giving you the peace of mind that eludes most business owners.

Enjoy the book and keep pushing yourself and your results...

Onward and upward!

Dr Marc Dussault
The Exponential Growth Strategist

Acknowledgements

Many people have inspired me over the years to my personal and business success. I would like to thank them for the help they have provided, some one on one and others through recordings or videos.

Business mentors and friends are many, but my marketing inspiration has come from a few select "gurus".

Jay Abraham gave us the inspiration to be creative and taught us marketing concepts and strategies to exponentially grow a business.

Dan Kennedy's help with sales letters and advertising is legendary. Dan's "out of the box" ideas have given our marketing personality and individuality.

Our newest mentor came by way of Australia, Dr. Marc Dussault has been a huge, practical technique inspiration. Marc has given us ideas we have been able to implement in our business, as well as helping our clients grow their businesses.

Henry Evans who pushed me to get this book written, thank you. Henry inspired me to complete a task that was sitting "on the back burner", and may have never been completed without his help.

Allison Hache my editor, someone who helped polish a very rough draft into the helpful book you hold today. Allison was patient yet enthusiastic about completing a project she also believed in.

"In business you've got to adapt, change or die. Whether you're on Wall Street or Main Street, everyone's goal is to increase the zeros on their bottom line. If you aren't including direct marketing to do that, then you're insane! Stop waiting for change to happen and let Eugene lead you the way to marketing success."

Jeffrey Hayzlett,
Host of C-Suite with Jeffrey Hayzlett

"Every business owner likes to chase shiny objects. Twitter this, Youtube that, and always looking for the magic bullet. But, the fundamentals never change.

Expert Eugene Montanez talks about how small business owners can use direct mail successfully in this timely book. I personally love direct mail and with email SPAM rates only going up, those business owners who realize direct mail is alive and well will do the best in this new economy."

Henry Evans
#1 Best Selling Author,
The Hour A Day Entrepreneur

Who Is Eugene?

If you are not sure why you should read or implement anything you read in this book, I wouldn't blame you. Most of the strategies in this book have been available for many years, if not decades. What I hope I have been able to do is to weave these concepts into a system you will utilize Direct Mail advertising to grow your business. My wife Paula and I have been working with business owners and managers for over 35 years, helping them increase their marketing effectiveness. Many of the ways we have been able to do this is with Direct Mail marketing. Over the last few years email and internet advertising have taken the headlines in marketing columns and books. But you will see in the book, many of these online companies use Direct Mail marketing themselves to reach potential advertisers.

During the last 35 years we have demonstrated time and time again that regular Direct Mail marketing does indeed work, and can grow any business or non-profit organization. During this same time frame, the same technology that has helped reduce the amount of mailings businesses do, has helped grow the ability to laser focus your marketing, to targeted recipients. Mailing lists can be purchased with data that helps you target to the exact audience you are trying to reach.

The fact that less and less people are using Direct Mail marketing, has actually now increased the effectiveness, since you are sharing less space in the mailbox with possible competitors.

Read this book, send me feedback after you have created a Direct Mail marketing plan, I would love to hear of your successes.

History

Modular Systems Printing...

was founded by 16-year-old Eugene Montanez in 1972, in his mother's garage on Dogwood Circle. With a small printing press, large paper cutter and darkroom consisting of a bedroom/bath combination, a printing empire was founded.

Corona Offset Creative Printing...

was created in 1976 when the business moved to its first retail location at the corner of 5th & Ramona, then into the back of the drive-thru dairy at 1541 West Sixth Street in 1978 and to 1441 Pomona Road, Suite 18 from 1979 through 1981.

Zap Instant Printing . . .

came about in 1979, and two "copy shop" satellites were opened: Southwest Plaza at Second & Hamner in Norco and 1307 West Sixth Street, Suite 127 in Corona. Quick printing technology brought a wave of growth in the industry, largely driven by desktop publishing in the 1980's, and business flourished. The shop was enlarged and remodeled, and the three locations combined to become Zap Printing & Graphics in 1981.

Zap Printing & Graphics...

grew from a retail quick printer/copy shop into a small-format commercial print operation, and relocated into industrial quarters, appropriate for a business-to-business service provider. In 1989, a gala grand opening was held at the new, custom-designed location at 223 Ott Street.

Corona Printing...

a long-time competitor and historic Corona business entity, closed in 2000, and Zap Printing & Graphics acquired the name and customer list. In order to maintain continuity, both names were used concurrently for several years. From 1993-2005 the business was located at 210 North Smith Street.

Allegra Marketing • Print • Mail...

In October 2005, Zap Printing & Graphics moved into their new building at 127 Radio Road. Constantly changing technology, along with growth and evolution from traditional printer to marketing services provider has fueled a decision to join forces with the Allegra Network. The business is now poised to provide a full array of graphic communication services, supported by traditional and digital printing and creative graphic design

Eugene & Paula Montanez ...

have been the co-owners/operators since 1976, and remain firmly entrenched today. Their deep roots in the community go back to their school days, with both graduating Corona High in 1973. Their record of community service is extensive, including Jaycees, Corona Rotary, United Way, Soroptimist, Boy Scouts, Chamber of Commerce, Library Foundation and more. Their son, Robert and daughter-in-law Angela are continuing the family tradition of local commitment and involvement. Robert has been a Corona Police Officer and Angela works for the department as a Community Service Officer.

Eugene expanded his commitment

to community in 2002 when he was elected to Corona's City Council after eight years on the Planning Commission. He served as Mayor in 2007, and began his third term on Council in December 2010.Eugene and Paula, along with their professional staff of marketing and graphic communication specialists and creative print technologists are always striving to fill a need in the local business community.

The Direct Mail Difference

The Definition Of Insanity

Every journey starts at the beginning, and that seems like the best place for us to begin. My best guess is that you picked up this book because you're ready to change your current marketing plan or to create an effective one for your business. Even if you don't understand why you feel the way you do, you know that you need to do something different. That's a good start. Einstein said that *The definition of insanity is doing the same thing over and over again while expecting different results.* Unfortunately, this describes many business marketing plans.

Chances are, if you've been in business for any length of time, your marketing plan is similar to others in your industry. If you're new to the small business game, you may be looking to more experienced business owners for marketing ideas. Unfortunately, in many cases, your industry has been following the same marketing strategies for decades without paying attention to whether or not they work. If they work, everything is great for everyone; if they don't work, you're all spending a lot of time and money to do something that doesn't help build your business.

Worse yet, you may have learned all your marketing strategies from college professors and experts who never had to generate enough money to make payroll each week. They write books and give seminars that give you tips for running your company, but they've never been forced to put them into practice with their names on the line. When the suggestions don't work out as they promised, they shake their heads and tell you that you didn't make all the changes you could have.

Unfortunately, most of these marketing plans are destined to fail because they lack metrics to measure if they are working. A marketing plan that works produces results through increased sales and profits, customer retention, and customer acquisition. If you can't determine if those metrics are changing, you don't know if what you're doing is effective.

Don't worry if you've been doing this. It's normal and is how most people market their businesses. However, today is the start of your new marketing journey. At the very least, I hope you start implementing changes in your current plan. Do something different.

In this book we will explore how you can use direct mail as a key component of your marketing plan. Direct mail offers you the ability to easily track your results so you know what is and is not working. It gives you the chance to experiment with different designs and formats so you can discover what works best for your clients, prospects, patients, or non profit donors.

I personally know it works because I have used it in my own business. We have operated a successful printing and graphic design business for more than 30 years. It has provided a great livelihood for our family, but we knew we could do better. We wanted to expand the company, hire more employees, and purchase a building. These are normal goals for any business, yet, the tried and true marketing ideas that we thought should work didn't get the results we needed to make these dreams come true.

A few years ago, we decided to join a national network. It was a huge step that forced us to completely revamp the business. We changed its name, sought marketing help through the network, and implemented the changes others in the group suggested.

Now, we're reaping the rewards from that long, hard transition to a whole new entity. It worked well for us, but none of it would have happened if we refused to think outside the box and try something new.

How to Use this Book

Change is scary, but if you want to see different results, you have to do something different. As you work through the process of creating a new marketing plan, you may be tempted to veer off course to try out the new ideas or beat yourself up for wasting so much time on ideas that didn't work. These are only distractions that take you on tangents and prevent you from working toward your goals.

Don't let these ideas sidetrack you. First, what seems like the best idea today may pale in comparison to one you discover later. Second, you can't change anything you did in the past, but you can learn from the mistakes. Keep notes in a notebook or digital document as you work through this book. This is a place where you can track your ideas, prioritize them, and create action steps and support systems to implement them.

Important

Take the steps today to change what has not been working. As you work, remember that the goal is to do something different so you can see different results.

There are Only Three Ways to Grow Your Business

Marketing guru, Jay Abraham, taught me a valuable lesson that changed the way I view my marketing plan. **There are only three ways to grow your business:**

* increase the *number of clients*
* increase the *average size of each sale per client*
* increase the *number of times each returns to buy again*

If you focus on these principles, you keep your sights set on growing your business and are less likely distracted by diversions and tangents. Best of all, you only have to remember three goals instead of 17 or 47.

Before you can begin, you need some information.

* How many clients do you currently have?
* How much money to do they spend, on average, on each transaction?
* How often do they purchase a product or service from you?

Let's say you have 1,000 clients who spend, on average, $100 per transaction twice each year. In this situation, you have the following formula:

Important

Only 3 Ways To Grow Your Business

* increase the number of clients
* increase the average size of each sale per client
* increase the number of times each returns to buy again

Setting Goals

Once you know what these numbers are, you can set goals to make them go up. If you increase each of those numbers by 10%, you increase your annual revenue to $266,200, a 33.1% growth. Increase those numbers by 25%, and your income doubles to $390,000. The arithmetic may be simple, but the results are overwhelming.

Increase Your Number of Clients

There are two ideas to keep in mind when considering how to increase your number of clients. First, above all else, you need to do everything in your power to keep the clients you already have. If you add new clients at the expense of the ones who already do business with you, you aren't increasing your number of clients. At best, your client base is stagnant, and worse, the number may decrease.

An effective marketing plan reaches out to existing clients just as much as it seeks new ones. Two-thirds of your business is already coming from existing clients. It's easier to retain them than it is to find new ones, making it easier to organically grow your business because they already have a relationship with you.

Implement an effective client retention program

This can be as simple as staying in touch with your clients and asking them how you can best serve them. You can also host client appreciation events and offer special discounts and promotions exclusively for them. These actions can go a long way toward fostering client loyalty toward you and your business.

Second, you have to find a way to increase your client base and transactions. This means you have to make sure you are constantly and effectively advertising and marketing your business to both current and prospective clients. I do mean constantly and effectively. It's easy to get complacent or distracted—especially when business is good—and cut back on promotional strategies. Instead, dedicate a portion of your budget for advertising and marketing efforts. Don't look at it as an expense. It's actually an investment in the future of your business, which translates to your future and the future of your employees.

You also need to find ways to attract new customers. Don't overlook the power of strategic partnerships or joint ventures with people in noncompeting, yet related businesses. For example, if you're a veterinarian, you could partner with the owner of a pet supply store and the owner of a pet grooming studio or spa. You can refer clients to each other and reach out to more people.

Increase the Size of Each Transaction

The second way to improve your business is to increase the size of each transaction, which translates into more money in the bank. This is called *up-selling*, and it happens everywhere from restaurants that want you to add a skewer of shrimp to your entrée to grocery stores that hope you will grab a candy bar while you wait in the check-out line.

It may not seem easy to convince your customers to buy more from you. However, you may be able to find products and services related to what you offer that your customers want to buy. Each new product or service translates to a new source of revenue, especially if you can convince your clients to buy the items they would purchase from someone else.

Beauty shops understand this principle. They sell more than haircuts and styles. They also offer cosmetics and other beauty items that are not necessarily related to cutting or coloring hair.

McDonald's also understands this concept. Before the nutritionists jumped in to warn the public about the dangers of excessive calories, everybody wanted to supersize their orders so they had bigger burgers, larger fries, and giant sodas. They did this by up-selling. For McDonald's, each sale was well over 10% of their existing sales (and probably closer to 25%). This simple up-sell transformed McDonald's business, and you can do the same.

Another way to increase your sales per item is to improve the *perceived value* of your products and raise the prices. For instance, if you're selling something for $200 and you're able to add true value to that product, you can sell it for $250 or $300, incrementally increasing the value of that particular sale.

Think about it. If you're going out to buy a car, do you automatically buy the cheapest one on the lot? Do you fall for the lure of heated seats, navigation systems, special lighting, or entertainment systems for the children? Each of these items has a perceived value that makes you willing to pay more for the vehicle. The dealer doesn't even have to twist your arm to do this.

Increase the Number of Sales per Client - -

The third way to build your business is to increase the number of sales per client. This means you need to get them through your door or on your website more often throughout the year.

The more you interact with your clients, the easier it is to convince them to come in and spend money at your

business. One way to do this is to send your customers postcards highlighting particular services that they may not know you offer. You can also send them newsletters to share with them success stories from other clients. This reminds them of what you have to offer and forces them to think about what products and services they are not taking advantage of. Ideally, they will then want to purchase them as well.

You should also take time to reach out to customers who are not visiting your business as frequently as they once did. They purchased your products for a reason, and you just need to remind them why they did ~~that~~. When you reactivate their interest, they return and increase the number of transactions you have.

As you work through your marketing ideas, stay focused on these three ways to build your business. When you consider new marketing ideas, ask yourself if it will increase your client base, convince them to spend more money with you, and get them to do so more frequently.

Half Of Your Advertising Is Wasted …

John Wanamaker, a 19th century general merchandiser once said, "I know half my advertising is wasted, I just don't know which half." The sad truth is that unless you are implementing marketing strategies that you can define and measure, your marketing and advertising efforts are also wasted.

There are no excuses for this. Modern technology has made it possible to track sales, responses, and leads much better than John Wanamaker was able to do. These tools optimize your marketing efforts so that you know what works and doesn't work for attracting new clients and retaining your existing customer base. This leaves no money wasted.

Why Branding is BAD!

Branding is the latest buzzword floating around at all the big marketing conventions. It is essentially institutional advertising, a way to put your name in front of the public in such a way that people instantly see and remember your name. What I'm about to say is controversial and goes against everything currently taught in marketing programs. If you don't believe me, do your own Google search of the phrase "when branding is bad," and you won't get many results.

The problem with branding is that it does nothing to actually increase sales, which is the way to increase your profits and your business. There's nothing wrong with having a strong brand, but it does not bring people through the door of your building or to your website. That's why it cannot be the focus of your marketing and advertising plan.

The History of Branding

You are already familiar with effective brands like Coca-Cola or McDonald's. However, these companies have something that you likely don't have: multi-million dollar marketing budgets. This gives them the leverage they need to continuously keep their names in front of their prospects so they reach for a Diet Coke when thirsty or stop at the drive-thru for a Big Mac when hungry. These companies have already invested much time and money to become the premier brands within their markets.

For years, ad agencies have used these examples to convince people (like you) that they need to invest their time and money building a memorable brand. Many companies have fallen for it because it makes them feel and good. However, feelings don't get results. Ask these ad agencies about the ROI on a brand. Ask them about the measuring tools they use to determine whether or not the branding campaign was successful. In most cases, they can't answer those questions because a great brand is an after effect of a great marketing plan.

Ad agency's emphasis on branding reminds me of the emperor's new clothes, if everyone keeps talking about it and looking at their "brand", eventually everyone will say, "Yes having a brand is the only thing to make my business stand out".

This does not mean you should completely avoid branding. Your company logo, USP, and even your facilities help you look good in the eyes of your clients. Your image is part of your marketing

plan. It just should not be its entire focus, and it definitely should not be done at the expense of other techniques that are measurable. When I work with clients, I make sure they realize my goal is to help them grow their businesses as quickly as possible. Creating and maintaining personal relationships with your customers will get you much further than having a "brand."

Instead of branding, another approach to marketing is direct response advertising and marketing. Instead of forcing them to only remember your name, it invites your customers to spend their time and money with your business. You can't track how easily people remember your name. You can, however, determine which advertising campaigns brought people through your door. If you can track the public's response to your efforts, you're not wasting your time.

The Direct Mail Difference

You need results for your company. You need to be concerned about sales and leads. At the end of the day, this is your money on the line, and you need to spend it on plans that will bring dollars to your company. This is why you should consider direct mail marketing.

What is Direct Mail? ---------------

Direct Mail is a form of *direct response* that tells your clients exactly what you want them to do. For example, if you want to let your customers know about a new service you offer, you can send them postcards announcing the service and how they can take advantage of it. However, instead of sending the information to everyone on your mailing list, you target the customers who are most likely to respond. You can even roll out the mailing in stages so you can test its potential success and know if it will likely work before investing a large sum of money.

Direct Mail is Not Junk Mail --------

At first glance, Direct Mail seems like a fancy word for junk mail, but it's not. Think about the so-called junk mail you receive every day in the forms of printed and digital messages. Some you read, and some you throw away. How do you choose?

You open the messages that appeal to you, and you throw away the ones that don't. Direct Mail uses technology to personalize the mail so you can make sure the message gets to the right people. The messages and images are carefully selected to appeal to people and organizations in different industries.

Direct Mail is High Impact ----------

Direct Mail is high impact advertising that gives you the most bang for your buck. It is a way to get information about your business to you customers in ways that catch their attention and don't cost you a small fortune. Best of all, it can be as simple as a postcard or complex as a company magazine.

Postcards	Sales Letters	Newsletters and Magazines
can be done in a variety of sizes, colors, and weights	more space to share special messages	range from 4 to 12+ pages
low cost postage	easy to combine with other marketing formats	easily customized

Direct Mail is Private - - - - - - - - - - - - - -

Another advantage of Direct Mail is that it's private. You are reaching your customers in the comfort of their own homes or businesses where your competitors cannot see what you're doing. This means you have the chance to attract their clients without them realizing what happened. You can also send different offers to people based on their interests and needs. Unless they talk to each other, they will never know that you are running multiple promotions. If they do, you can always offer the same deals to them.

Direct Mail is Inexpensive - - - - - - - - - - -

Direct Mail is inexpensive when done correctly. That's right! As long as you target your audience and use an effective call to action, you can rest assured that you are spending your marketing budget wisely in the avenues that will give you the best ROI.

Here's an example. Imagine you mail 1,000 postcards to your clients in three different stages. If you spend $1,500 to produce and mail all the postcards and get 30 responses from them that net 10 sales worth $250, your net return is $2,500.

This is an even greater number when you consider how much each client will spend over the course of a lifetime. Even if the initial campaign brings in less than you anticipated, it still might be worth the effort if you gain just two lifetime customers from it. If those two customers bring a lifetime value of $100,000 to your company, you netted $98,500 from a $1,500 investment.

People Like Mail

Another key fact is that people like mail. Mail is tangible in a way email can never be. It evokes emotion and delivers a message that you care enough to use your valuable time to send it. People receive mail every day, and 72% of them bring in the mail as soon as they get it. 56% of them say receiving mail is a real pleasure, and

55% actually look forward to discovering what treasures wait in the daily mail pile. If that doesn't convince you, remember that 67% of the general public believes that printed mail is more personal than email. You want to have a personal relationship with your customers.

Businesses also still like mail. When a business is evaluating products or services, they prefer mail versus email, and 69% of them prefer direct mail that is targeted and personalized for them. Compare this with the 28% who prefer email and the 3% who want a telephone call.

Why You Should Use Direct Mail

In today's technology-driven world, some people think online advertising is the only viable advertising for reaching clients. Perhaps you, too, have sent a message or two through the social media powerhouse Facebook. Yet, you probably don't know that Facebook actually spent over $200,000 on Direct Mail in 2012.

I've received mailers from Google, Yelp, and other online firms. They could do all their advertising online for free, yet they choose to use Direct Mail as part of their marketing plans. If online advertising really is the best way to reach out to customers, why would these companies spend millions of dollars on direct mail? It's simple. They know the value of putting something tangible in the hands of their clients.

The advantage of Direct Mail is that it is guaranteed to get you five to seven seconds of one-on-one time with the recipient. They cannot fast forward through the message, delete it with the click of a mouse, or change the channel. Your message is in front of them. It may be only for the amount of time it takes them to deposit your postcard or letter in the trash, but you at least have that distraction-free time with them.

That amount of time, no matter how small, is all you need to see a conversion. Think about your own daily routine. You see those postcards. Don't you ever keep any of them for later? Have you ever contacted a company after finding a message from it? If you have or will respond this way, you can expect others in your target audience to do the same.

It Works for the Little Guys, Too - - - - - - -

I have seen firsthand the power of Direct Mail compared with email. One of my clients, Orange Mud, wanted to expand its retail business to include a wholesale division. Josh, the owner, decided to look for new wholesale clients using only email. The response was lackluster, so Josh agreed to let us mail postcards to his 700 name mailing list. They mirrored his other print and online materials.

The first set of postcards arrived in the clients' mailboxes on the Fourth of July, a holiday weekend. Yet, surprisingly, Josh immediately received phone calls. He had been tracking his email campaign and knew it had a 0.003% response rate. The very first postcard produced a 3% response rate during a holiday weekend when his clients were taking time off.

Online companies know that they cannot rely solely on online media themselves, and you should follow their lead. Remember that Google can advertise on Google for free, so the fact that they use direct mail to grow their businesses should show you that you need to pay attention to the power of direct mail and not discount it as an outdated advertising method.

Does Direct Mail Really Work? (You're Still Not Convinced?)

Consider the following:

* 24% of adults who read direct mail visit and do business with the mailer within 90 days.
* Customers who receive a catalog spend, on average, $39 on the company websites. Customers who do not receive a catalog spend $18.
* 84% of Generation X and Y members (the digital generations) read and keep direct mail.

How Direct Mail Works

Jay Abraham and Dr. Mark Dussault often talk about the power of exponentially growing your business. To do this, you focus on one step at a time, building one piece on top of another.

Direct mail helps you do that. You already know the three ways to build your business, and you can implement a direct mail plan to target just one of those goals.

Visualize your direct mail marketing plan like a puzzle. You work with one piece at a time (like increasing the number of clients), and once it is in its place, you move on to the next (like increasing the amount of each sale). Eventually, you notice completed sections that help you work faster to complete the puzzle. In this way, you exponentially improve your efforts.

When you apply this approach to your marketing plan, you are able to grow your business exponentially. Direct mail is just one part that, when used effectively, makes it easier to work the rest of the plan. You walk a mile one step at a time, covering more distance as you move forward.

How to Make Direct Mail Work for You - -

At the end of the day, you're in a business or practice that requires money to keep that business or practice going and the only way you're going to have that income is to have continual response. You can implement direct mail as part of your plan to do just that.

Increase Attendance at an Event

You can use mail to increase attendance at an event. Whether it is a formal event sponsored by your company or a casual Lunch and Learn, or networking event, mail is a powerful way to get the message out and fill the seats.

Marketing for a Trade Show

A mailing is also a great way to get in touch with your customers and partners to let them know about upcoming trade shows. You can send the mail before the event to invite them to participate and after the event to increase your response.

Increase Website Traffic

There's no denying that a well-designed website is a useful business tool, and you can use mail to direct people to the site. People who visit the website are far more likely to buy something than the people who don't visit. This is actually what Google and Facebook are doing. It's just another medium to advertise their primary business.

Solicit Donations

Of course, non-profits need donations in order to survive. They can use direct mail to solicit these donations. It's much easier to get your message across through a written response that is actually in the donors' hands. This is even more powerful when they are forced to look at the faces of those they will help printed on the sales letter.

Direct Mail and Trade Shows

To attract attendees to trade show booths as well as a regular printed newsletter to client and prospects.

Eugene: Thank you for taking time out of your busy day, if you could tell us a little bit about your company and what your company does.

CC Vest: I'm CC Vest and I'm President and co-owner with my husband of an industrial distribution company called Midpoint Bearing. We have locations in Ontario, California; Converse, Texas and Oklahoma City, Oklahoma.

We've been in business 29 years come 2014. We've grown by leaps and bounds last five years.

Eugene: What kind of industry do you serve?

CC Vest: We're an industrial distribution center with our niche market in electric motor and pump repair. We specialize in bearings and accessories for electric motor repair facilities across the country.

Eugene: Basically, you supply to small companies, large companies ...

CC Vest: They can be all the way across the board. We handle OEMs to small repair shops. We also handle repair facilities that do the wind generators across the country.

Eugene: One of the things that's always impressed me about your company is the wide variety of marketing medium that you use. One thing that I know you're very regular in producing is a newsletter. How long have you been producing the newsletter?

CC Vest: Let me see if this is Volume 6 Number 17. So a bit over 6 years now, on a regular basis.

Eugene: How often are you producing the newsletter right now?

CC Vest: We do them quarterly.

Eugene: One of the things that I know other clients that we've talked about doing a newsletter, they have a concern about the amount of time it takes. One of the things that's impressed me about how you've designed your newsletter in blocks so you know you get a piece from somebody and another piece from somebody else so it doesn't seem, to be an overwhelming task for you.

CC Vest: We planned it that way on purpose. The cover sheet is basically what we feel is important to the times. Dan writes it. I review it. I give him the ideas and he sits down, pens it and then he comes to me and then we banter back and forth and then we do share the other things.

We hired an engineer last year so he gets a section and then we share with our vendors so that we can bring new products to keep the spotlight because the pictures that you put in the newsletter, they speak volumes.

Pictures are just so much more for our customers in the industry that they serve because you can be too technical in words but until they see a picture they can't piece it together.

Eugene: I think with photos in any kind of advertisement, it makes it easier to scan and creates an immediate interest, drawing your reader to a particular topic.

CC Vest: Right. We can even put some pictures from our phones now. They're so clear now. It's amazing. We couldn't do that before. We can have real time pictures. I can be at a convention, take pictures, send them to Allegra and Debbie, your artist can start working. It's fabulous the way that works. We do that every year and we put her in that position and she always comes through for us.

Technology has moved everything into the next level. Something that I'm not techie and this will be the year where I'm moving away and letting my younger people step into the limelight for the social media, having gone to the classes that you've done.

They're going to have the bright ideas. They're going to be the ones that say this works, this doesn't work. People my age are just moving out of the industry. They're only going to come to me for technical things now.

Eugene: Do customers and clients comment when they get the newsletter?

CC Vest: Absolutely. Absolutely. They look in the newsletter. They also send it on Constant Contact so they can archive it. Some people just ... they scan it and they'll save particular articles. Our engineer provides technical information the customer can use for reference.

Eugene: It's something that they can quickly review but get some actual education from?

CC Vest: Right. A lot of people use that in their own training. If we find that there's problems in the industry with certain things, take a look at this ... bearing with poor lubrication ... this is what happens ... this is what to look for and then they say, "Darn! That's what's happening." Or electrical arcing or anything like that, they didn't know the technical terms. They didn't know what they were looking at. They were just thinking that's just a failure and a failure's a failure but there's always reasons for bearing failures.

Eugene: That helps tie you directly to the client, makes you a valuable resource to them too.

CC Vest: Exactly. It's Christmas and I'm seeing clients that I've had for 30 years. I'm getting Thank You cards. Thank you for all the help you've given me. Thank you for getting me through the hard times. If it wasn't for you, I wouldn't have the client base that I have.

It's really important for me to hear that because it makes it all worthwhile.

Eugene: One of the other things that you do, and you mentioned a little bit about trade shows, I think what makes you unique is you really sweat over the details about what you do a theme. You really work at trying to get your clients and prospects to the show.

What is your goal? What are you trying to do? What kind of things do you do that you found to be successful?

CC Vest: We always have a mailer we do to have the clients bring to the show. When they do, we take them to a specific area in our booth to show them the specials that we have so that they can actually get demos on site and then also, perhaps, via the reduced prices. Our vendors usually contribute to that effort and they get one-on-one time with them at the same time.

Eugene: I think that's a big plus because I know a lot of people will go to a trade show, set up a booth, expect people to come to their booth, just throw their checks or their credit cards down and say we want to buy but you actually go that extra distance and do the promotion ahead of time to get people to the booth.

CC Vest: Exactly. You saw the poker chips. We used lots of the chips and it was really fun to pass them out. We also had a lot of promos that you did for us. I'm still giving them out for Christmas actually, my jar openers that are always with me. Those kinds of things. People like giveaways. People like functional giveaways.

Eugene: I think one of the things that we have really been trying to emphasize is promotional items like what you're talking about is to make sure you can use it to theme in for a show or for an event but if you have extras, they still have your name on them, you can be using them for other events or, like you mentioned, for holiday gifts and add-ons when you go see a client.

CC Vest: It's very male-dominated industry so it has to be a workable, usable item. Things have changed over the years. Some things are just not important.

Eugene: You also do calendars every year as well as one more touch to your clients?

CC Vest: Yes. We have decided that the most functional part of the calendar is our year-at-a-glance where you can, the erasable ones that you do. The smaller calendars are just almost non-existent anymore because people's work spaces have gotten so small. Our vendors co-op with these and everyone's logo is printed on the calendar.

We try and bring everybody to the table so it's not just money we are spending. Everybody benefits, the major brands we supply get the exposure.

Eugene: I think anybody that has co-op money from vendors, they're silly if they don't utilize all the opportunities co-op money can bring to the table.

I think what also sets you apart is that you have a broad product selection but you offer consultation and help to clients where the "really big guys" will maybe have the same or better inventory but they're not going to walk a client through a specific problem.

CC Vest: We treat every client the same. I saw a customer today. I've known him for many, many years, 35 years actually. He said, "You know, I know you have bigger customers and you still make the time to come and see me."

Eugene: Exactly. You mentioned now you're moving in to adding on more email marketing, more social marketing.

CC Vest: Right. That's not even me, that would be Amy. She will be creating the new efforts in email and social media.

We did our numbers and we've already surpassed last year and were up last year.

Eugene: Thank you very much.

CC Vest: You are welcome.

Direct Mail As Drip Marketing

Drip Marketing is a process of automatically sending relevant information by email or direct mail over a period of time. You "drip" the information based on either user action or a pre-defined time interval.

Important

> To do this, segment your clients and prospects into categories. Prepare and send to them different messages through a process of five, ten or fifteen touches. You can use letters or post cards to share the information.

Say, for example, that you want to get 100 new clients. You can send to these prospects alternating letters and postcards. The first may be an introductory letter with a sales message about your company or practice. Thirty days later, you can follow this letter with a postcard one. The following month, you can send another letter. By the time you send a second postcard 90 days later, you will have sent out several drips of information and can convert the prospect to a sale. Project this to a six month or one year period or shrink it to fit in a shorter time frame. Combine this with personal calls by your staff to reach higher response levels.

It's easy to modify this strategy to fit your needs. If you have email addresses for your prospects, you can incorporate that format into the plan. Just don't make email the only format you use. When combined with direct mail, you will see a greater response.

These actions can be automated quite easily and delegated to internal staff or outside partners. If you use it effectively and with consistency, you should be able to increase your sales with existing clients as well as prospects.

Drip Marketing is also useful to reactivate previous clients who are no longer visiting your business, buying from you, or donating to your cause. By using this multiple touch approach and incorporating it with a newsletter campaign, you remind these previous clients why they used to do business with you and why they should again.

It also works before and after trade shows. You should already know which clients are likely to go to a trade show or networking event. Send out two or three mailers prior to the event. If you're able to get trade show attendee information from the show promoter, send out promotional information to them as well.

Don't limit the contact to before the show. The most important and least utilized benefit of any trade show or networking experience is contact after the event. You can implement a drip marketing campaign at this point to remind the customers that you were at the show, thank them for attending, and encourage them to do business with you.

Like with every other marketing strategy we recommend, make sure you track the results. You may experiment with different sequences or copies of letters. You may lengthen or shorten the drip campaign to find out what length of time is most effective.

Your Customer As An Asset

The three ways to grow your business have one common component: the customer. It is extremely important that you understand how valuable your clients are to your business' success. Face it, your business would not exist without them.

The Lifetime Value of a Customer

To get the bigger picture of this, look at the number of active clients you have and the average gross income you earn from them. Multiply this number by the number of times they will do business with you during their lifetimes.

This number helps you decide a few things. First, it helps you budget how much money you are willing to spend to get a new client. If the lifetime value of a new customer is $5,000, would you spend $50 to get that customer in your pipeline? Would you spend $100?

Second, it helps you set the threshold of what you are willing to spend to get and keep your customers. (Chances are that once you understand what you stand to make from your clients, you will be more likely to expand that threshold.) With this information, you can make informed decisions about how you will spend your marketing budget.

Knowing the lifetime value of your customer gives you more flexibility when you spend money to attract new clients versus when you try to retain existing ones. If you know your clients will continue to contribute $500 per year to your business every year, your marketing will likely be much different than if you only look at an average sale of a $100. If that same customer will be worth over $5,000 over the lifetime they remain in your pipeline, that customer can be a true asset who will be happy, return to buy more, and refer others to you.

The lifetime value of a customer can change over time as your business and industry evolve. In our business, we continue to offer more and more services in house. The lifetime value of our customers and clients has increased exponentially since we're able to satisfy more and more of their business needs. We started out offering simple printing and an occasional rubber stamp to our clients. That slowly evolved into two color and four color printing services, signage, and poster and banner printing. Not only has the lifetime value of our clients grown, but our prospects have changed, as well.

Originally, our prospect was any business, and that was kind of a shotgun effect. We had no way to know who was most likely to do business with us. Now we target our prospecting to medium and large businesses.

Acquisition vs Retention

By now you realize that marketing is about more than attracting new business. It's also part of retaining the clients you already have. Most business owners concentrate all their marketing efforts on attracting new business. Yet, it's the most difficult way to do grow. It's much easier to increase the amount and frequency of your current customers' transactions than it is to find new ones. Review the formula for the lifetime value of a customer. If you only conduct business with new customers, you miss out on all the money you could make over the course of a lifetime.

Your marketing plan needs to have two specific levels: acquisition and retention. Your acquisition plan is based on what you want and are willing to do to acquire new clients. However, you also need to consider what you are willing to do to keep those new clients so you can later cash in on their business. To do this, you have to form relationships with your clients so they know how valuable they are to you. Newsletters highlighting your products and services, customers' stories, and employee updates help build and maintain those relationships. Postcards offering special offers to loyal customers have a similar effect.

Important

Remember, it's more costly and more time-consuming to acquire new customers than it is to retain the ones you already have. This doesn't mean you should ignore new clients. On the contrary, you need new clients to build your business. Just keep that in mind as you work through this process that your priority needs to be retention. Acquisition is always secondary to retention.

Raving Fans

One special group of existing customers is especially important to the success of your business. Entrepreneur Dan Kennedy calls them raving fans, and he tells business owners that they need herds of these fans following them. Raving fans are customers and clients who have a passion for you, your staff, and your products. They love to see you grow and prosper because they believe in what you do. These raving fans are most likely to continue doing business with you and refer all their friends and family to your company as well.

You must create and sustain a herd that loves you and your company. You have to make a personal connection with them and smother them with great service and products. The deeper you form that personal relationship with them, the more they will rave about your firm.

One of the goals of your total marketing program is to turn your clients and patients into raving fans. They will grow your business or practice faster than any paid advertising ever will. Once you have them on your side, they cost you nothing and will continue to bring new business your way. Raving fans are also an asset that your competitors will never know about, and they cannot do anything to steal them.

Take the time to take care of your raving fans by talking to them one-on-one. Let them know that they are an integral part of your success, and make sure that you always provide them excellent service. Look for ways to reach out to them through direct mail.

Use Newsletters to Build a Fence and Protect Your Herd

Every business loses clients each year, and this is usually because of apathy. If you don't stay in touch with your clients, they begin to think you don't value them and will look to your competitors to meet their needs. It is especially important that you protect your raving fans. You need to build a fence around them that keeps them near you. A good newsletter is one way to do this.

Newsletters are excellent tools that separate you from your competitors. They give you a way to talk to your clients on a regular basis in a personal way that makes a connection. In each issue, you have a chance to talk to them about your business, give them tips to improve their lives, and show that you are in business to meet their individual needs.

Great Newsletters Give Practice Information -

You can design your newsletters to educate your clients or to promote products and services. However, I normally recommend that newsletters avoid hard sells. They are intended for the people who are already buying from you. Instead, you can use the newsletter to highlight products and services that your clients don't currently use or to announce new items to your lineup and how other clients are using these products. In this way, it is a third party endorsement for what you offer.

Great newsletters are also fun to read - - -

Remember that this is a way to connect with your clients. Let your personality shine through the content. Share your favorite recipes or holiday rituals. Highlight fun events that happen within your community or industry. You can even keep them up to date about what is going on in your personal life. Business relationships are nurtured through personal connections.

Great newsletters are consistent - - - - - - -

This means that you need to send it out consistently. The only way to do this is—you guessed it—to have a plan in place.

Be as detailed as possible and set deadlines. Perhaps you will write it on the first of each month, collect photos by the tenth of the month, and find an article from a vendor by the fifteenth. You can send it to your design team by the twentieth so it can be assembled, printed, and prepared for mailing before the end of the month. A regular system like this keeps the process continuously moving so you don't even have to think about what to do next, and your customers won't miss out on the content you're providing.

One of our clients sends out a monthly newsletter. It is a four page, full-color document packed with information. Each month, the company owner and one of their vendors write a column. The rest of the newsletter is filled with photos and captions. It is simple, yet effective because it strikes a balance between business and personal information.

If you really want to take over this process yourself, we can help you put together a shell. Then you only have to enter the information each month. This will help maintain consistency in the design, which will increase your clients' familiarity.

Regardless of how you approach the newsletter production, make sure you start doing it. It is such a simple way to improve your customer retention. You simply cannot put a price on the "face time" you get with them each month. This lets you cement the relationship you have with them and create lifetime customers who are loyal to you. In terms of investment, newsletters can generate a much higher return than trade publications, online ads, coupons, and other mailers.

What makes newsletters so successful is the same quality that works with direct mail. As companies shift their marketing to digital and online formats, they leave open a space for you to do something different that will let you stand out.

Newsletters to block competition and grow a real estate farm

Tara & April Glatzel – "The Sister Team"

Eugene: Thank you for taking some time to discuss the newsletter you producce, can you tell us a little about your business?.

Tara: What do we do, we sell real estate.

Eugene: How long have you been selling real estate.

Tara: It's all I've ever done since I was 20 years old. That's all I've ever done, April joined me 16 or 17 years ago, and that's when we became a sister team.

Eugene: One thing that you guys have done though, is you target a very specific niche area of homes, right?

Tara: Yes, we work in the Wood Streets, and a real estate term that everybody uses in real estate, is called farming, you're cultivating a farm, like a farmer does. You plant the seed, and water it, and it grows. That's what we do in our neighborhood. We just pass out that newsletter in the hopes that when somebody needs a real estate person, they would think of us when they need our service. We do newsletters, we do Fourth of July flags, we do candy, we do notepads, we do seed packets on Mother's Day. We do all kinds of things. We try to get something out once a month, in the hopes that again, when somebody needs a real estate person, they would think of us.

Eugene: Can you explain a bit about the newsletter?

Tara: These are printed are a huge, huge, part of our business.

Eugene: On the newsletter, how long have you both been doing a newsletter.

Tara: It says it on our newsletter. I want to say it's almost ten years. I think last year ... eight ... Oh my gosh, it says it on our newsletter, I think. It's eight or nine years.

Eugene: It says happy 11th birthday.

How often do you print the newsletter?

Tara: It varies. We try to do it once a month, but this past year ... it just varies, probably on the average of every other month. We had somebody that was trying to swoop into our neighborhood, so we really upped up our game the last couple of years. We just did ours in December. We're probably going to skip January, just because I just don't think we're going to get around to it. Then we always do a February newsletter with our Love pops for Valentine's Day, so we'll definitely do that.

Eugene: Now as the economy slowed over the last couple of years, I think one of the things that impressed me, was seeing that even if you cut back a little bit, you both continued to push your marketing.

Tara: Yes.

Eugene: Was that something that really helped in your mind to keep your business going within your farm area?

Tara: Absolutely, yes, because when you pull back, you'll actually hear people, even if you just skip a couple of months, because we're gone on vacation, or it's August and it's 120 out, because we do it ourselves, we do it door-to-door. People will be like, "Where's the newsletter?" They look forward to it, and they really like reading it because our's ... it's fun, we think. It's not boring. We try to put fun little things in there, and people really like it, and if we skip months, people really miss it, so it's really important to be consistent.

Eugene: I think because your farm area is the area where you're working and living, and I think one of you lives within the farm area too, right?

Tara: We both do, actually.

Eugene: Okay. You actually put information in the newsletter that's relevant to the neighborhood, and I think that's something that helps a lot too.

Tara: Yes, absolutely.

Eugene: One of the concerns, that people have when we recommend they look at doing a newsletter for their business is that they say it takes too long to put together. What have you been able to do to make it easier to do, and do on a more regular basis.

Tara: I can not take any credit for it. April does our whole entire newsletter, and she works really hard on it. I could see that being a complaint, because if I didn't have her I don't think I would be able to do it. There are many services out there that would produce and mail a newsletter for you. Or copy and artwork you can take to your local printer.

My broker always said, "It doesn't matter what you give them, just give them something on a consistent basis", so it doesn't necessarily need to be as personal and cutesie-pie as we do ours. It can just be a standard newsletter on whatever somebody's business is, but consistency is the key.

Eugene: I agree that you have to have consistency, but I think having something in your personal voice, and showing your personality, goes a lot further. I know I've received some of the canned newsletters from realtors and other mortgage brokers, and they just look the same. They're just not interesting, and I think that's really what makes yours different. You've got information about your neighborhood. You have information about homes for sale, neighbors like to know what is happening in their neighborhood. You tie in the articles to be more thematic for the time of the year. It really shows a lot more personality of the two of you.

Tara: Yes, I absolutely agree, but if people don't have the energy or an April, she works so hard on it and if somebody couldn't put something together like that, something is better than nothing. The couple that was trying to cut into our neighborhood, if you will. Their newsletter was not good or personal. It just was terrible. Hopefully I think they finally have gone away, because we haven't seen them for four or five months. People say that all the time, it's just better, and you guys are head and shoulders above the rest. It did help to have a more personal newsletter that people actually do like to read.

Eugene: It helped too that you had many years in the neighborhood and the farm area before the new people showed up. It would take them a period of time to really be able to make any inroads.

Tara: Exactly.

Eugene: I think some of the other things you mentioned, about all the other touches that you do, are most of those included with the newsletter or do you do those as separate handouts when you're in the neighborhood?

Tara: Pretty much everything's in our newsletter, although sometimes we will do a separate, "just listed", or if we do an open house, we sometimes will send out open house invitations. I think you guys have done that for us in the past.

We've been so consistent with our newsletters, if there's something coming up, we'll putting it in there, like our "Cookies with Santa" is this Sunday, that's why I'm baking right now. We'll probably have hundreds of people come to do our "Cookies with Santa", so we just put that directly in our newsletter, but if for some reason something's coming up and we don't have a newsletter, we'll just print it and then throw those out in between the newsletter, but pretty much the newsletter, we put everything in there.

Eugene: I think it really shows through. When I noticed that you were still producing it during the slow times, I was certain that would carry you through the down time. A lot of people, when things slow down, they cut way back, and then it's harder to re-enter the market, to get top of mind, in your case, a farm area, and other businesses within their prospects and things.

Tara: Absolutely.

Eugene: Thank you.

Tara: You are welcome.

Your Direct Mail Road Map

How We Implement a New Marketing Plan for a Client

When we have clients who are serious about growing their businesses and implementing new marketing plans, the first thing we do is sit down with them and talk. This is a brainstorming session that can include anyone the owners want to bring.

Step 1: Gather Data and Develop Ideas - -

We start the meeting by exploring the business itself. As we talk with the owners, we learn about the current and past successes of the business, what has worked in the past to increase business, and what has not worked. This information helps narrow the focus to find a marketing plan that will get results.

Next, we talk about the business' competitors. We explore the various industries they work in and discuss ideas the competitors have used that they would like to try as well as those they never want to consider.

Finally, we talk about the business goals. We need to know how they want to grow the business and what segments they want to develop. In addition to this, we talk about whether or not they want to stick with only their existing clients, reach out only to new customers, or work with a combination of both. We even discuss marketing ideas and projects they have always wanted to try but never got around to implementing. As we talk about ideas, a mini marketing plan emerges.

In most cases, this conversation is a completely new experience for the owners. They spend so much time running the company that they don't stop to really examine where they want to take it and how they can get there. However, this information is vital to creating a marketing road map.

Once we have all the basic information we need, we help them create a plan that increases the numbers of sales, leads, and customer retention. Then we move on to generate ideas for how to do this.

Step 2: Prioritize Ideas - - - - - - - - - - - - -

At the next meeting with the client, we share the ideas we developed and sort them according to how much they like or dislike them. From here, we use the budget and timeline to prioritize the marketing plan so we can be sure to put into action each segment of the plan at the right time.

Step 3: Implement Ideas - - - - - - - - - - - -

The real work begins at the next stage. We schedule the graphics and mailing list purchases (when necessary). At this point we also design and develop other presentation and promotional materials, like presentation folders for sales personnel, point of purchase material for dealers, in store signage, and promotional products. This entire process is planned in a way that effectively utilizes promotional products and maximizes ROI. Once this is in place, we start the mailing stages.

We carefully time mailings for maximum effectiveness and repetition. There should be no delays between each segment, but they should also not overlap. In most cases, we plan a campaign that covers a six month time frame. This gives the clients time to send multiple messages without seeming too pushy.

I hope you see the progression of the steps. Notice that the campaign does not begin with a haphazard mailing to everyone on the existing list. No one designs a single postcard until we've talked about goals and clients and competitors. Instead, it is a carefully planned series of actions that work hand in hand to produce the biggest results.

As excited as you may be about monitoring and enjoying the results of the work, you must go through the process in a step-by-step manner. This is the most effective way to do this. Take the time to carefully set everything in motion. Once the initial system is up and running, you can let it move on autopilot while you focus on implementing other changes to help grow the business.

Why Would You Market Your Business Without a Plan?

Chances are you have never gone on vacation without some sort of plan. At the very least, you chose a destination and picked a way to get there (by a plane, train, or automobile). Without a plan, you run the risk of losing out on your hard-earned money and time.

Important

> This is also true when developing a marketing plan. Even if you have the best idea ever, you shouldn't attempt to implement it without a step-by-step campaign. This campaign is a carefully planned balance of the right attitude, realistic expectations, and an effective action plan.

Attitude is Everything: Finding a Sense Of Urgency

Imagine your dream vacation. Think about what you are willing to do to make it happen. Chances are, you would work extra hours, clip a few more coupons, or skip your morning lattes for the opportunity to relax on a tropical island or hike in the mountains. When you really want something, you do what you have to do to make the dream a reality. This sense of urgency forces you to get started on the steps and complete them as quickly as possible so you can reach your goals.

A Sense of Urgency Keeps You Focused on Your Goals

The real achievers in life don't necessarily have the highest I.Q. scores, best education, or most money. They have this sense of urgency. Look at the lives of the most successful and productive people throughout history, and you will see that they were in nearly constant motion. They knew their goals and worked to achieve them. They did not accept setbacks and disappointment as excuses to quit. To achieve your goals, you need this same sense of urgency so are willing to do whatever it takes to realize them.

A Sense of Urgency Helps You Set Measurable Steps

You also need measurable steps that track your progress from where you are now to where you want to be. It's easy to get sidetracked when you have no way to see your progress toward the bigger goal.

Each New Year, people claim they want to quit smoking, lose weight, or spend more time with their loved ones. Most of these resolutions are forgotten before the end of January. Why do you think so many New Year's resolutions fail? They wanted the results, but they lost faith along the way. Real change takes time. If your eyes are only on the end result, you may fail to see everything else going on that is leading you toward the goal.

For example, someone may want to set a resolution to lose 50 pounds. It's an admirable and achievable goal that will change your life. However, it will take time. Most experts recommend that you should lose one to two pounds per week. That means it will take between six months and one year to see this happen. That's a long time to wait.

However, if you set measurable milestones to mark your progress toward the greater goal, you will give yourself the encouragement you need to keep going. As long as your milestones are part of a well-crafted plan, you can keep your focus on the short term to boost your enthusiasm and watch the plan work on its own.

A Sense of Urgency Prevents Procrastination

When you know what you want and how you will get it, you can prevent procrastination. Procrastination has killed millions of great ideas. Not only does it destroy your sense of urgency, but it undermines your entire plan. Don't give in to the temptation to put off the work you need to do. Set deadlines and attack the process in small bits and pieces that will eventually add up to bigger results.

Be specific when setting deadlines. Look at what you have to accomplish, and break it down into smaller, manageable steps. These steps should be specific, like, "Brainstorm with the staff on Tuesday" or "Brainstorm with friends over lunch on Friday." Share your goals and deadlines with your trusted associates so they can help you stay focused and on track. This added accountability will increase your sense of urgency. Join a Master Mind group to help keep you motivated and focused on your goals.

I've had to work to develop my own sense of urgency. For years, I have wanted to write a book. Marketing is one of my passions, and I want to share what I know with others. I just never got around to even putting together a plan to make it happen. Then I met with a group to help me put a book together. We set deadlines that gave us peer pressure to force me to get the book completed on time.

A Sense of Urgency Helps You Pay Attention to Your Efforts - - - - - - - - - - - -

This sense of urgency also helps keep you from repeating the same mistakes that are not getting results. When you know you have to do something, you won't be as tempted to let your ideas sit on your desk where they will never see the light of day. Knowing that your simple actions can make such a huge difference in your life will help you stay committed to change.

Your sense of urgency will also force you to track and rate your campaigns and make the most of your efforts. The results you get will encourage you to keep working to find what works and multiply those results. You won't want to waste your time repeating the ideas that didn't work.

A Sense of Urgency Helps You Prioritize - -

Finally, your sense of urgency will protect your personal time. It's easy to let yourself get overwhelmed with everything you have to do. If you use the sense of urgency to set deadlines and make your plans come to fruition, you will have more time to spend doing what you love with your loved ones.

Realistic Expectations

Your dream vacation can never happen if you don't have enough money to cover the expenses. A month in French wine country may be fun, but brown-bagging your lunch for a week won't get you the money you need for that trip. The same is true of your marketing efforts. You need realistic expectations so you can see actual results.

One Percent Improvement

You might be surprised to learn what you can accomplish if you add one goal or task to your life each day. If you improve that single task by 1% each day, you can double the results every 70 days. When you apply this to your business, you will see exponential growth and achieve your ultimate goal in record time.

Amazon put this concept into practice. It is a huge company, but the executives are always looking for ways to incrementally increase customer service, sales, and profits. In 2006, the company released the results of an astounding study on the relationship between website speed and revenue. After reviewing its website and making minor adjustments, it was able to increase revenue by 1%. When you have a gross revenue over $60 Billion, 1% adds up to some nice pocket change.

The lesson here is that it takes just a small effort to bring large results. Think about the projects you're working on now. Approach them in small chunks and do the best you can in each moment. This leads to constant improvement which will keep moving you forward.

Other companies have used this concept as well. Near the end of 2008, Zappos sent the following memo to its employees.

"We can reminisce about 2008, but now that 2009 is here, and we are back from some much-needed downtime, it's time to get our A-game back on.

We'll be going over our goals and our "official plans" as soon as our board approves them, but even before that officially begins, we already know what we need to do. One thing I encourage you to do is to refer back to our core values document and specifically the challenge in there. Make at least one improvement every week that makes Zappos better. Ideally, we would do this every single day. It sounds daunting, but remember improvements don't have to be dramatic. Think about what it means to improve just 1% per day and build upon that every single day. Doing so has a dramatic effect and will make us 37 times better, not 365%, which is 3.65 times better at the end of the year."

"Wake up every day, and ask yourself not only what is the 1% improvement I can change to make Zappos better, but also what is the 1% improvement I can change to make myself better personally and professionally, because we Zappos can't grow unless we as individual people grow too. Imagine yourself making 1% changes every day that compounds, and will make you and Zappos 37 times better by the end of the year. Imagine if every employee at Zappos was doing the same, imagine how much better you, Zappos, and the world would be next year."

You can follow the examples set by Amazon and Zappos and seek to improve just 1% of your business model. Like compound interest, that effort—no matter how small it seems—can skyrocket your business.

No Quick Fix

As you set your realistic expectations, you must keep in mind that no marketing plan is a quick fix. You will have to plan. You will have to work. You will have to pay attention and adjust the plan as needed. This isn't a difficult process, but it cannot be rushed.

You cannot proceed with a direct mail campaign thinking it will be a quick fix to your marketing woes. It's always possible, but it takes time and repetition for your ideas to stick with your customers.

We recently met with a dentist who wanted to acquire 500 new clients in six months. Was it possible to do this? Of course. Was it likely that this would happen? Of course not. He did not have an unlimited budget, nor did he have the desire to work through a comprehensive plan. He was looking for a quick, easy fix that would generate massive amounts of business without much effort.

Instead of hoping for miracles, you need to make plans for three months, six months and one year. Know where you're headed and plan your mailings well in advance. It's much easier to coordinate your message this way and to keep yourself on track with a schedule and deadlines.

However, this doesn't mean you are stuck with these plans. You are completely free to make changes as you move forward. But, like taking a road trip without having a road map, you'll never get to your final destination without some idea of where you're going. Even if you do, you'll get there in a very circuitous route and waste a lot of time and energy. Your direct mail campaign and your marketing in general is exactly the same.

Massive Action Leads to Massive Results

After you have cultivated your sense of urgency, you have to put it to good use by exercising massive action. You cannot half-heartedly attempt to work through each stage of your marketing plan and expect to see massive results.

You're reading this book because you have ideas in your head and project notes on your desk that you want to see become a reality. If they stay where they are, you stretch the amount of time it takes to reach your goals or, worse, do nothing and stay in the same stagnant place.

Important

> Once your goals are in place, start working through each step in your action plan, using your sense of urgency to propel you forward. After you complete an action, evaluate the results and make adjustments to later steps as needed.

Your plan is never set in stone and can be modified as much or as little as it needs. Review it. Work with it. Test it. Use the information to decide what to do next. Never let the plan sit on a desk or computer file gathering dust. It wants to be put to use in a massive way.

Your commitment to massive action will get you out of your comfort zone. As you watch the results come in, your drive will be invigorated, and you will be encouraged to do even more. You will want to prepare your direct mail campaigns ready to go and work with your provider to implement everything you planned. Massive action makes everything better.

Unless you plan for it and you go through all the steps, you will have wasted time and energy. Plan for results. Plan for your business to grow. Plan for the future, knowing full well that it is a multi-step process and it will take some time to achieve your goals. You don't have to finish all the steps as you read the book, but you do need to make sure you're aware of where you stand in the process.

Find the Right Method to Get Where You Want to Go

The right attitude and expectations do not make a great vacation happen. You also have to find a way to get there. This is also true of your marketing plan. You need to find a way to get your message to the people most likely to buy your products and services. Unless they buy, your time and money is wasted.

People Buy From People

Despite the nature of the industry you're in, the types of customers on your mailing list, or the business model you have created, you have to make a personal connection with your clients and prospects. You're not selling your products and services to a business or residence; you're selling to a person. Making a purchase is an emotional decision for your customers, and they need to trust you in order to make that happen.

Your mailing is going to a person, not a business or residence. The message and media you choose needs to reflect this. You have to consider each person's gender, income and education level, and buying habits. Each of these factors helps determine the type of message you want to send and how you send it. For example, younger prospects will almost always expect you to direct them to a website for more information. Women are usually more willing to read all the information in your mailing, while men often prefer to look at only the headlines. Knowing this helps you craft your message as well as how to deliver it.

Speak the Right Language

The more you know about your target prospects, the better equipped you are to talk directly to them. When you do this, they are more receptive to your message because they feel like you're speaking their language and understand how they think and feel.

As you design a message for your target prospect, picture that ideal client in your mind. Imagine that you are writing directly to that person. In some cases, you may need outside help for this. For example, if your target prospects are considerably younger or older than you, you may need the help of employees and associates who are in those age ranges. They will likely be better equipped to find the right language and talk on that demographic's level.

Just remember that personalization is important because your message is going to a live human. You need to make sure that your materials are written in language that will resonate with them and uses a format that they are comfortable with.

You Know Where You Want to Go; Now Make it Happen

There's a reason Americans traveling overseas are more likely to eat at McDonald's than a local restaurant. It has little to do with the sight of the golden arches or an innate love of fast food hamburgers. They know what to expect on the menu and how the food will taste. A local restaurant cannot guarantee this "safe" experience, and McDonald's knows this. The restaurant has a system in place to ensure this happens.

An Effective System is No Accident

The McDonald's operation system was designed by two brothers in San Bernardino, California. They put together an automated system that made it possible for 16 to 18 year olds to run a multimillion dollar business with limited adult supervision. It is simple and efficient, with step-by-step procedures for doing everything in the restaurant, from making hamburgers to cleaning equipment.

Important

McDonald's has a system that works.
The food is not premium quality, but you know when you see the golden arches along the side of the interstate that you can find a clean restroom and eat a quick meal. You also know that a McDonald's cheeseburger is prepared and tastes the same at any restaurant in the country.

Although the system was put in place decades ago, it has been continually modified as the wants and needs of the customer changed. Yet, the system is still central to the production and success of the company. The system actually guarantees a pleasant experience that makes people return to the establishment.

Effective Systems are Easy for Anyone to Follow

The McDonald's system teaches us a lesson about implementing our marketing plans. If the system we design is complete and follows a step-by-step process, we can invite others to help us. It also helps us stay on track because we don't have to constantly remember what to do next. This efficiency makes us more productive. Keep this in mind as you develop and implement your own plan. Think of the people who will need to complete tasks on a daily, weekly, or monthly basis. Then make sure that the plan is systematic so they can do their jobs.

Perhaps you don't have an in-house staff that will help you implement the tasks. A system also works for contractors. If your system is already in place, you can explain to them exactly what they need to do. Having these detailed instructions makes life easier for both you and the contractors.

For example, if you decide to use a drip marketing plan, you need a system that ensures your letters and postcards go from point A to point B and point C. Each step in this type of system must be carefully timed and arranged in advance so that everything is ready to go on the first day of the campaign. If the system is designed correctly, you can put it motion and forget it. In fact,

that's the secret to any successful system. It should run automatically without unnecessary supervision.

Effective Systems Let the Customers Know Exactly What to Expect - - - - - - - -

McDonald's isn't the only business that has carefully designed systems. Amazon's entire business model incorporates a highly developed automated system for processing orders. You only have to click the BUY button on the website. The company sends you a confirmation email, and as if by magic, you receive the order within a few days. You can even track the order as it is being processed and know exactly where it is within the country. Soon you may have your Amazon merchandise delivered by a drone!

Yet, there's no magic involved. It's all the result of step-by-step planning and a functioning system that ensures each step will be completed in a specific way.

If you follow the same concept and implement a predictable, reliable step-by-step system, your customers will notice. This consistency goes a long way toward improving your customers' awareness of your company and building their sense of loyalty to you. You want them to think of you and ONLY you when they or their friends need to do business or donate to a cause. An effective system makes this possible.

The Road Map To Your Marketing Plan

Unless you really enjoy side trips and looking at the scenery, you need a road map to help you get where you want to go. When you use a road map, you start by finding where you are. Then you compare that with where you want to go and explore the possible ways to get there.

Before you start designing your system, you need to examine your current business situation. Talk to your employees and clients about their visions for the company and what they think you do well and what you could do better. Ask and answer questions until you have a complete picture of the state of the company.

Marketing Attempts

* What have you historically done with your marketing?

Print Materials

* What printed marketing material do you have?
* How often have you changed it?

Website

* What does your website or websites look like?

* Were they professionally designed?
* Was the copy written and reviewed by a professional copy writer?
* Does your website have lead capturing landing pages?
* Does it have offers for a free report or video?
* When was the last time you updated your website?
* Do you use your website and online tools in conjunction with your other marketing efforts?

Office Personnel

* If you have sales staff, what presentation materials do they have when meeting with clients and prospects?
* What instructions have you given the front office staff to help them answer prospects' questions?
* Do you have an assistant to handle calls, emails and personal visits?

Trade Shows

* Do you have a plan for appearing at trade shows and networking events?
* Do you contact clients and prospects before show?
* Do you have a real plan for the show?
* Who do you target and what do you hand out?

* Do you have a plan for displaying promotional materials at shows and events?
* Do you have a total integrated plan for your promotional products to have them tie in with your marketing plan in general?
* What follow-up procedures do you have for events?
* After a trade show, do you mail follow-up information to any prospects that stop by your booth?
* Do you get all attendee information from the show promoter, so that you can follow-up with prospects that may not have left information with your staff?

Competition

* Do you have their printed marketing materials from your competitors to compare to yours?
* Have you examined all their websites and online presence?

Important

Once you have completed and written your plan, post it in a place where you and your staff will see it on a regular basis. Everyone on your team needs the constant reminder of what the plan entails. This is your road map and will help you stay on the road to success without costly and time consuming side trips.

Your Marketing Tool Kit: You Already Have Everything You Need, You Just Have to Find It

You're in your business because you love it. It makes your customers happy. It gives you pleasure. It provides for your lifestyle. You just have to take a close look at what you offer so you can let the world know and share in your joy.

What Makes You Different: Determining Your USP

The first step in your new marketing plan is to determine your company's unique selling proposition (USP). Jay Abraham taught me how to develop and use an effective USP, and I want to share that with you. This USP identifies your business and differentiates it from your competitors. It tells your customers why they should come to you instead of everyone else who offers similar goods and services. If you want people to spend their time and money at your business (or professional practice or non-profit), they need a reason to do so.

It's a simple concept, but creating one that works is not a quick process. The best way to do this is to consider what is NOT a good USP. Simply saying that you have good service doesn't tell your customers how you will help them. It certainly doesn't show how you are different because every company claims to have great service. It's also not enough to come up with a cute slogan. Cute slogans are fun and ideally help your customers remember you, but they are not USPs.

USPs Create Industries

USPs are powerful and have helped define entire industries. For example, for years people and companies have delivered packages for us. They were reliable companies that moved our packages from point A to point B. Then FedEx decided to beat these guys at their own game. Instead of just delivering our packages, they were willing to get them to their destinations overnight. FEDEX' industry changing USP was: *"When it absolutely, positively has to be there overnight."* That USP let their customers know how FedEx was different from the U.S. Postal Service and UPS. USPS responded by creating their own overnight delivery service, and the express delivery industry was born.

USPs Tell Your Customers Why They Should Choose You

Remember, USPs tell your customers what makes your business different from every other business in your industry. Dominos Pizza did this when it announced, "We deliver hot, fresh pizza to your door in 30 minutes or less, or it's free." Notice that the USP doesn't say anything about the quality of the pizza. It doesn't claim that they have the best pizza, use Mama's secret sauce recipe, or make the pizzas with the freshest ingredients. It says that they will get the pizza to your house faster than anyone else. That's what made them different from their competitors.

Dominos not only created this delivery market; they owned it. Pizza franchises across the country now follow the same procedures. Even Pizza Hut, the industry's leading player, was forced to rethink its strategy of building sit-down pizza restaurants across the country. Now, the bulk of their business is based on takeout locations.

Find Your Shining Star: Create Your Own USP

Important

Now that you understand what a USP is, you might want to know how to create one? Remember that this process takes some time, so it's okay if you don't figure it out right away. By the time you finish this book, you should have enough information and ideas to create your own USP.

With that said, don't let the fact that you don't have a USP stop you from developing your marketing plan. Yes, you need a USP, but it doesn't run your marketing campaign and can change over time as your plan develops.

Talk to Your Customers

Start the USP creation process by talking to your customers, clients, patients, or donors. Ask them directly why they choose to do business with you. This insight is invaluable and lets you know what edge you already have over your competitors.

Talk to Your Employees

Next, talk to your employees. Schedule a 30 to 60 minute staff meeting. Ask them what they offer your customers. Brainstorm ideas, writing down each one. At this stage, no idea is a bad idea. It is also important that you include all employees in this process. This means everyone, from office personnel to salespeople and back room personnel should be in this meeting. They all have different perspectives about what makes the business work and why they work for you. You need to know this because it will give you more ideas about what makes you different from the competition.

Talk to Yourself

Finally, consider why you would buy your goods or services. Before you can sell your product or service to the public, you have to sell it to yourself. Chances are that you're not a one of a kind business. What do you offer that all the other retailers, manufacturers, hardware stores, air conditioning installers, and electricians don't have? How do you want others to see you? Charles

Revson, the founder of Revlon cosmetics understood this. He told people that he sold hope, not makeup. Likewise, some airlines sell friendly service. Others sell on-time service. Southwest Airlines sells free baggage and no change fees.

What Do You Really Offer?

Keep your focus on your company and the policies you have that benefit your customers. Use this insight and look for common themes that you can turn into a USP. Look for something that really conveys why a new customer should look at your company and say, "Oh, they're different. I should try them." To do this, the USP needs to be as short as possible while telling the complete story about what makes your business different.

Once you think you have a USP, look at your competitors. Make sure you are doing something completely different. Refuse the insanity of following the same tired policies that are not working. Be willing to evolve as you need to. Your job as a marketer and business owner is to reach out to your clients in the most effective way possible. That way might be something completely unheard of to your competitors, and it might make all the difference for you.

Your USP will be the foundation of your marketing and will make it easier for you to implement it. It will be part of the work you do with direct mail, networking, and trade shows. When you meet others at these events and pass along your business card or brochure, they should see the USP. If it's effective, it will stick in their minds. Chances are that your competitors have not taken the time to develop their own USPs, and that gives you a distinct competitive advantage.

Work through this process and use the accompanying worksheet in this section to help you develop a great USP.

Standing Out in a Sea of Choices: Sending the Right Message

You have a plan. You have a USP that shows what makes you different. Now you need to get that USP in front of your customers so they know why your company is so great. However, it's not enough to just state that. You have to do so in a way that catches your prospects' attention and gets them moving in your direction.

Adding Character and Personality

We have yet to meet the person who runs the only business within a single industry. McDonald's, Burger King, and Wendy's all compete for the same customers. So do Toyota and Honda. You, too, have competitors who are vying for the same customers you want to attract. Worse, they really want to take your existing customers and make them their own. This is why you have to do whatever you can to make your company stand out from the rest.

Why Me?

At the heart of your campaign is the USP that tells your customers why you are different. You don't have to dress in crazy costumes, give away cars, or come up with a catchy phrase (but you could do that if you want). All you have to do is let the customers know why they should choose you.

Start by thinking of your own purchasing habits. Where do you shop? Why do you continue to do business there? What makes you decide to try a new business? Something caught your eye that made you willing to walk through the door or visit the website. Look for ways you can incorporate the same qualities in your own business.

Give Them Something

One way you can distinguish yourself in your direct mail campaign is to offer a free report. It can be a report about insider information in your industry, details of a cause you believe in, wellness advice, or any other information you think your customers will find useful.

You can use your postcards or newsletter to direct people to a landing page on your website where they can get the free information. However, the landing page serves an additional purpose. Before sharing the free report, you can prompt the visitors for more information, including their email and physical addresses, phone numbers, and even demographic information like age range or gender.

This helps you measure the success of the campaign because you can verify the addresses on your mailing list and check demographic information. If you had hoped to target women between the ages of 25 and 34, you only need to do some simple calculations of the visitors' information.

Look at Me!

You can also distinguish yourself by doing something wild and crazy that your competitors would never be willing to do. If you really want to go to the extreme, there's an interesting book by Bill Glazer called *Outrageous Advertising That's Outrageously Successful*. Like the title states, some of the ideas are quite outrageous, but others can be toned down for a more subtle approach. If nothing else, it will give you some ideas to get you started.

Just be aware of how the public views your industry. Some industries, like cars sales, are perfect for crazy gimmicks. In fact, many customers expect this. Others, like professional practices, work better with a personable approach. You may buy a car once every three or four years, but you have your teeth cleaned annually. As a result, you develop a closer relationship with the dentist than you do with a car salesman (who may not even be there by the time you buy your next car).

Having that one-on-one relationship with your client or patient is paramount. Your mailing materials need to have a conversational tone that does not seem like a sales pitch. Instead, you should talk to them like you are close friends. This will go a long way toward making sure you are the first person they think of when they need to schedule an appointment or refer friends.

All Offers Must Have Deadlines

Important

You already know that your mailing material must have a call to action that lets the customers know what you want them to do. It's just as important to have a deadline for the response. Your prospects need to know when the offer will end.

Deadlines Tell Your Customers That the Offer is Important

When your offer is available for a specific time, it sends the message that your offer is so compelling you will be inundated with new orders. Your customers know that you are serious.

Deadlines Help You Plan Your Mailings

Make sure that your direct mail piece has the deadline that corresponds with the deadline you give your customers. You don't want them to receive the mail after the offer has expired. Consider that the Post Office may take up to two weeks to deliver bulk mail (which is now standard mail). Keep this in mind when choosing the day to send out your postcards or mailers, and make sure the deadline falls after that two week mail processing and delivery time.

The delivery period may not be as long if you are sending your mail pieces to local addresses, but it's better to be safe than sorry. After you've done a few mailings, you'll get a better handle on the delivery times and will know exactly how much time you need.

This emphasizes how important it is for you to carefully plan each step of the process. If you find yourself in a time crunch and need to get the mail pieces out sooner than bulk mail can deliver, your only option is to send the pieces through First Class mail. This option can easily double the cost of your postage and take a chunk out of your marketing budget.

You Don't Believe Me? Talk to These Satisfied Customers: The Power of Testimonials

Testimonials are powerful. These small snippets, quotes, or featured stories let prospects know others are pleased with your products and services. They build credibility and give customers confidence that they will have a similar experience with you.

You should, ideally, have a long list of testimonials as a resource for your marketing pieces. Always use actual names and resist the urge to quote anonymous testimonials so they customers know the quote is from a real person.

It's actually fairly easy to get testimonials from your clients. Just ask them for one. Keep asking for testimonials until you have enough. If you have trouble getting these quotes because your clients are too busy to write about their successes with your company, you can take a poll. A rating system takes little time for them to complete and still shows what they like most about doing business with you.

Put this information in a binder or digital folder so you utilize them as you need to in your marketing plan. At each stage of the development process, review the testimonials and choose the ones that are most appropriate for your marketing material.

You can include these testimonials in your sales letters, postcards, and landing pages. Testimonials have the greatest impact when you are reaching out to potential customers, especially when the prospect personally knows the endorser. They can verify the information in a phone call or at a social occasion.

This illustrates why it is important to create your raving fans. They are most likely to give you testimonials that let their love of your company shine through. Your raving fans also know how to speak to your clients in customer-speak, a language they all understand. This is some of the greatest sales verbiage you can use.

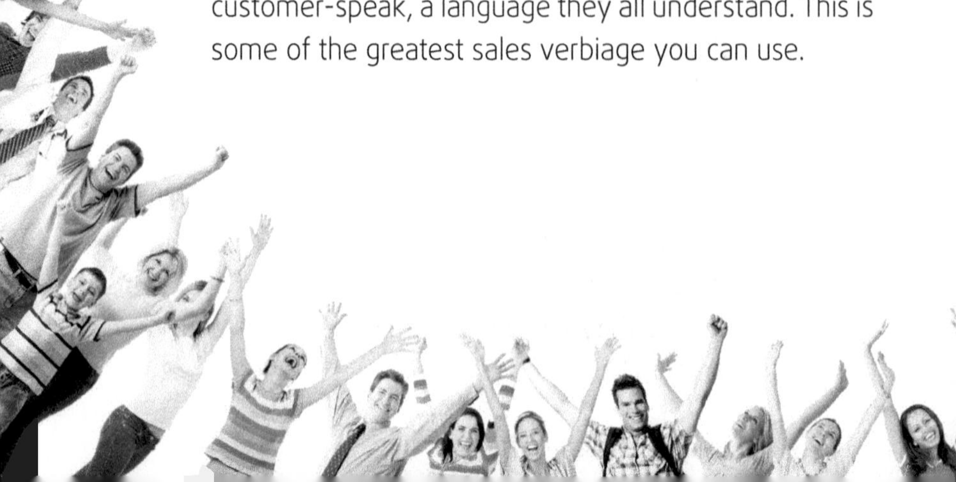

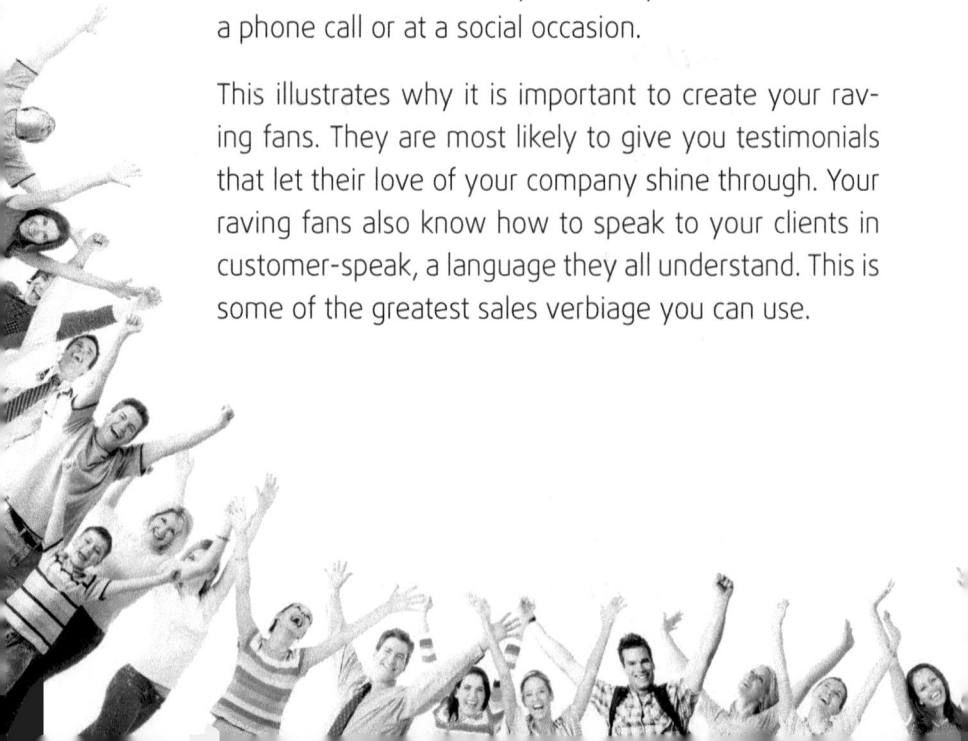

A Method in the Madness: How to Send Your Messages

Once you know what you have to offer and are ready to share it with your prospects, you need to know how you're going to do it. Remember that direct mail tells your customers exactly what you want them to do. You should have this in place before you begin.

Landing Pages Give Your Prospects a Destination

A landing page is a website that exists solely to give or obtain information. If you use the Internet, you have undoubtedly visited many different types of landing pages yourself. Sometimes you're aware that you're looking at a landing page. Other times it's not so obvious. Most landing pages are not sales sites because they don't selling anything. Instead, they are lead generation tools that ask your customers to supply information.

The best landing pages offer your customers white papers, a discount coupon, or educational information. Sometimes they also direct clients to outside sites after they have provided information the company needs for their marketing plans.

Your direct mail marketing (and e-mail marketing, for that matter) should direct clients to your landing page. An effective page represents your business, is simple to navigate, and gets to the point.

This starts with a captivating offer. Whatever you decide to give the customers in exchange for their personal information has to appeal them. At the very least, you want them to share with you their names and email addresses so you can measure the success of the campaign.

This only works if the process is simple for them to follow. If the page is difficult to navigate or you ask for too much information, the prospect will leave your site immediately. Remember that the purpose of this page is to convert the web traffic to leads and, ultimately, to sales. Get the information you need and let them move on. You can always follow up later with an email or direct mail piece.

Ideally, you have in place a system that automatically downloads information from your landing page into an auto response system. You can then set this up to trigger the next stage in the process, to automate your lead generation process.

Landing Pages Help You Track Results - - -

You can also use landing pages to test your marketing. For example, you can send out 5,000 postcards to your target prospects, directing half of them to one landing page and the other half to another. This will help you determine how effective your landing pages are and fine tune them in order to get the greatest response.

If you're worried that a landing page is a waste of resources because it's not actively bringing in revenue, remember that 95% of people visit a website before buying. They have no intent to buy at that point. In many cases, they are only looking for contact information, using the website like the yellow pages. It's not a waste if you are able to keep your name in front of them and gather information that will help you improve your communication with them.

Using Email Marketing to Your Advantage

It may seem strange to discuss email marketing in a book about direct mail. However, I know you can't help yourself. Email marketing is the new standard for business promotion because its quick, it's cheap (if not free) and easy. Just remember that you get what you pay for. Don't assume that because you hear others using email marketing that it is effective. Think about how many times each day you hit the delete key in your inbox. If the subject line doesn't catch your eye, you never look at the content.

I personally know two people who do not have computers on their desks. They have someone else go through their email every day and pass along important information. They miss out on some special deals and offers, but it's not worth the pain and hassle they experience sorting through the emails on their own. I do envy their system, and the distractions they avoid every day.

However, you can use email marketing in conjunction with your direct marketing. You need email addresses for your long-term business growth, and one way to get those emails is through direct mail. Use direct mail to send prospects to your landing page where you can gather this information. In exchange, give them a free gift, information, or coupon.

Once you have your prospect's email address, you can schedule an email to complement direct mail pieces. Email is just another tool you can use to test the responses you receive from your marketing campaigns. To do this, you need to know how many mail pieces were sent as well as you click-through and open rates.

Just don't let email marketing be a shiny object that distracts you from more effective techniques. Use it, but do so in a way that boosts your total plan.

Social Media is Just Another Tool in an Effective Marketing Plan

Many businesses have included social media, especially Facebook and Twitter, as part of their marketing plans. It's another way for prospects to contact them. If you are already doing this, you need to find a way to incorporate these formats in your plan.

However, social media should not be the primary outlet for your marketing. It is a specialized format used by specific groups of prospects. If your prospects are not using social media, the time you invest in it is wasted.

There's nothing wrong with having internet paid ads, but it doesn't make sense to spend money advertising in any medium if it doesn't increase sales. The reality is that web advertisement is not always as effective as the advertisers would like you to believe. Buying an ad on Google will not raise your Google ranking. Buying an ad on Yelp will not guarantee you increased exposure. Some of these programs are easy to sign up for and seem like logical ways to reach out to more prospects, but they may not be the most efficient use of advertising dollars. If you can not track your results and determine your true ROI, avoid them at all costs.

Consumer businesses such as restaurants and retail stores typically have the greatest success with social media. They use it to offer discounts, coupons, and loyalty programs for their regular customers. On the other hand, professional practices like medical offices and law

firms do not see similar success. In some cases, participating on social media detracts from the perceived professionalism and makes prospects question whether or not the practice is qualified. Carefully look at the characteristics of your target prospects and determine whether or not the y will respond to social media before you invest your time and money.

If you plan to integrate social media with your direct mail and direct marketing campaigns, do so wisely. Don't let it distract you from your ultimate goal or meeting the smaller deadlines along the way. You want to concentrate your efforts on the places where you are most likely to find your high value clients.

Like with all your other marketing ideas, test the response you get from social media. Look at the responses you get from those campaigns. Repeat what works. Stop doing what doesn't work.

What's That Shiny Package? Using Lumpy Mail

There are two types of mail: flat mail and lumpy mail. Lumpy mail, sometimes called 3-D mail, is anything you receive that has a dimension to it, packaged in a padded envelope or box. Lumpy mail can be anything from a ballpoint pen to a toy soldier or a little plastic trashcan. You can include brochures, samples of your products, or any fun item you want to send.

Shock and Awe

Dan Kennedy calls larger box promotions "shock-and-awe" packaging because it can result in such a high return, especially with larger lifetime value customers. If that prospect is worth thousands of dollars per year, what would you spend to acquire that customer?

I talked to a real estate agent the other day who mentioned that they have a targeted clientele of people selling homes worth more than $750,000. When they get a lead on a potential listing, they deliver a box to the prospect's front door. In the box is a bag of tortilla chips, a bottle of salsa, a six-pack of beer, and some information about themselves. This is a powerful message to a client who has not agreed to spend even one dime with the company. It will leave an impression that will last for some time into the future. The options and ideas are endless for shock-and-awe packages.

Making Lumpy Unique

Think about your own mail. What have you received recently that was different from your usual mail? What elicited a response from you? Other people will likely respond the way you did. If you felt it was a negative experience, don't repeat it since someone else may feel the same way. If you laughed, you may want to try it yourself. Getting a prospect to laugh when they get your mail is priceless.

If you are thinking about lumpy mail, think outside the box. Do you have a physical product ties into to your service and could be sent through mail? Have a little fun with it. Write a personal message to connect with your prospect on a one-on-one level. Just make sure the message also fits with whatever item you include. For example, you could send prospects foreign currency that might be worth $.25 as a way to attract attention. It's catchy and colorful, but it needs to connect with the message in your sales letter.

Lumpy mail is expensive because it costs more to ship than postcards, newsletters, or sales letters. However, imagine that the lifetime value of your customer is $10,000 per year. Spending five to 10 dollars to send that package is well worth the effort.

Promotional Products are More Than Gimmicks

In our line of work, we frequently meet business owners who want to purchase pens, coffee mugs, and other promotional items as a gift for clients and prospects. They think that just giving away these items is a sufficient marketing system.

You can probably guess how we respond to such generic requests. Spending money without a plan to measure success is a waste. We cannot, in good conscience, support such ideas. Anyone can—and does—randomly hand out these freebies, so it hardly makes your company seem different.

However, when you combine the use of promotional materials with a well-thought-out plan, the freebies can themselves be a marketing campaign. In this case, you are looking for responses to the gifts.

For example, if an event is happening within your industry or your town, you can make an arrangement with the person planning the event. Offer to give pens and scratch pads to everybody in attendance. Your material is then in front of these prospects, and you are the sole advertiser. You can then measure the effectiveness of this campaign by tracking the number of people who later contact you because they saw your pen and scratch pad. Better yet, have a response card or link to a landing page to get immediate, measurable results.

Promotional Materials Work Hand in Hand with Your Marketing Campaigns

You can also use promotional materials to enhance your marketing. Look for places in your action steps that give you opportunities to give items to your prospects.

We recently produced a few hundred hand sanitizers for a client who wanted to hand them out at a trade show. The colors and designs were planned to match his marketing campaign. It was a simple idea that was highly effective because the tradeshow was geared for teachers. In case you don't know this, teachers use a lot of hand sanitizer in their classrooms. Our client was able to track the response to this tradeshow and watched it meet his expectations because the overall plan was carefully designed and executed.

This experience also taught our client a valuable lesson. A few weeks after the show, he received a call from a teacher. The teacher was interested in the client's product and wanted to contact him but could not find any recognizable literature about the company. However, the teacher did remember the hand sanitizer and found the contact information printed there. As a result, he made a sale that brought his company thousands of dollars.

You have an almost limitless number of promotional products available to you. In fact, anything that you can print your logo on is a promotional item. Just remember that you don't want to use these items only for the purpose of putting your name in front of your prospects. That's branding, which is not measurable. You also want to make sure that the promotional items have your contact information printed. They need to be tools your prospects can use to find you.

Consider how you can incorporate promotional materials in your marketing plan. You can mail them to clients and prospects, ask your sales personnel to give them away, or offer them as free gifts for people who visit your landing page. Look for thematic ideas within your marketing plan. For example, if you are selling a new type of water filter, offer a reusable water bottle as a gift. If you sell computer products, give away USB flash drives. When you tie your promotional materials with your products and plans, you get twice the mileage out of your marketing.

When we help craft your marketing plan, we can also create promotional product plans you can use for your target audience. This will help you get the maximum return on your investment in whatever product you choose.

You Can Stop the Insanity and Know What's Working for You

The best laid marketing plans are a complete waste of time if they don't work. Fortunately, it's fairly simple to test and track your results so you can repeat what gets results and leave everything else in a marketing graveyard.

Tracking Your Results

Before you can track your results, you have to have measurable data. This starts with a useable mailing list packed with important demographic information. You will use all of this to craft your messages and send them to the right people.

Don't Try to Market without a Custom Mailing List

You need data about your customers so you know how to determine your target prospects. Like it or not, there is a wealth of extremely detailed data available about each one of us. Looking at this data sometimes feels like an invasion of privacy. However, this detail is what makes it possible for you to decide which customers are most likely to respond to your mailing. It's there, and you cannot erase it. You might as well use it to your advantage.

A Good Mailing List Tells You Everything You Need to Know about Your Prospects - -

Mailing lists are the life blood of your direct mail campaign. In fact, the list you use is far more important than the design of your mailer or your offer. If you send the most beautiful postcard with an offer no one could refuse to the wrong person, you are only wasting your money.

This is why we will work with you to determine which names on your house list are your target prospects. We can also procure mailing lists that will maximize response rate while testing it within different demographics or matching your current client base.

You can purchase lists in large or small quantities, and a list with as few as 500 addresses is a good starting point because you can target multiple micro targets within that group. Usually, I recommend buying a list that is the size you eventually want to mail once you know which materials are best to use. You can save money this way since you don't have to keep buying multiple lists and can still send out test mailings.

When working with a business list, we can target specific data such as SIC code, industry type, number of employees, annual sales, executive names, and phone numbers. If you want to work with a consumer list, the data available is even more personal. You can select from information such as the number and age of children in the house, income and education levels, home value, types of credit cards, and much more. This information will help you measure the type of response you get, based on the particular demographic chosen.

We can also review that list, remove duplicates, and run it through our database of the Post Office's National Change of Address (NCOA) database. This database will help us ensure that we have the most current information so we can minimize waste and save money for printing and postage costs. Like the orchestra conductor, we make all the individual pieces work together.

This is just a fraction of how we can help you make the most of your mailing list. By micro targeting your mailing campaign, we can assure your mailing is customized for those target prospects.

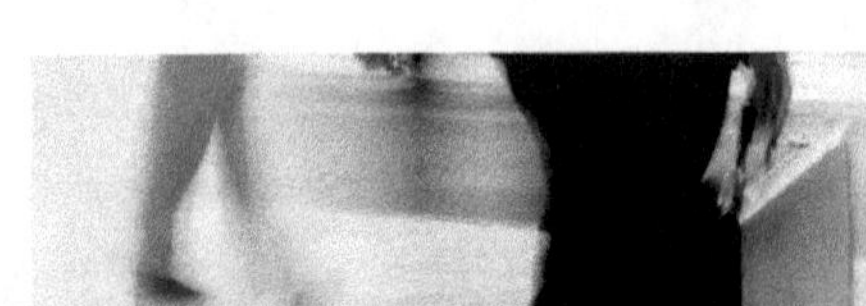

Strong Mailing Lists are Laser Focused Marketing

Although direct mail seems like an outdated marketing method, many of the steps it uses can be enhanced by the use of technology. You can use technology to point a laser on your target and determine who your prospects will be.

You don't need to mail everyone on your list. Instead, you can target a certain segment that you think is most likely to benefit from what you offer. You may want to concentrate on clients who have visited your office or website but have not purchased anything. You can even focus on attracting new customers.

This is why demographic information is critical. When you can focus a laser beam on the list, you can spend your time and money only on the customers you want.

With split testing, we divide a mailing of 5,000 postcards into two or more mailings. This lets you see how effective your offer is. For example, you can send one postcard out on January 1, a second on January 20, and a third on February 15. In less than two months, you have completed three touches to the market segment you are testing. Repeat this as many times as you need to fine tune your marketing message and demographic information so you know if you're on the right track.

Be willing to evolve your list and practices as you move forward. Keeping that laser focus in mind will help you grow your business at the fastest possible speed.

Your Mailing List is the Key to Targeting and Metrics - - - - - - - - - - - - - -

At this point you understand why you need to carefully target prospects and create materials that will appeal to them. Technology has made this easier than ever. However, you also have to test each action you take, each mailing you design, and each system you used to target your recipients. These metrics will let you know what really is and is not working. Remember, you don't want to keep using tools and strategies that don't get results.

Measuring your response rate is the only way to know if your mailing was successful. Otherwise, you're relying on your gut feelings and can only little more than "My sales are up (or down) this month." You cannot use such a vague statement to determine what to do next.

You want your marketing plan to be effective, and you need numbers that you can work with to plan future campaigns. As you test different versions of materials and different lists, keep track of the following details:

* How many prospects did you get to your landing page?
* How many prospects visited your website?
* How many prospects called your office requesting more information?
* How many emails did you receive?
* Did your sales staff contact the prospects to convert them into new clients?

You can keep this information on a spreadsheet that lets you easily sort information into different categories. For example, you may want to see if a particular mailing date was more successful than another. Perhaps you want to know if a specific postcard received more responses from men or women. You may even want to know what type of offer brought you the most leads.

When you can measure how prospects respond to your marketing efforts, you have all the information you need to make informed decisions. If you want to target women for a certain product or service, you can review your data to find out which type of mailing, time of year, and communication format was most successful in appealing to them. In the long run, this will save you time and money.

Don't Play with Secondhand Information. Go Right to the Source and Interview Your Clients

Important

Numbers are great to work with because they are easy to manipulate and give you a starting point for setting your goals. However, your clients are also an excellent resource for information about what you're doing well and how you can improve your products and services. You need this feedback on a regular basis and should check in with the customers you personally interact with as well as the ones who only talk to your sales personnel. There is no substitute for this personal interaction.

Be Genuine -

Show them that you care about their lives and their successes. Have a list of questions ready to ask so get similar information from each of them. Ask how their businesses are doing, how your company is part of their success, and what they like about the way you do business. You also need to ask how you can improve their experience with you.

Be Specific -

Ask them specific questions about your marketing efforts. You need to know if they have seen your materials and what they liked and didn't like. Don't be afraid to ask about your competitors' marketing as well and what interactions they have had with them.

Be Sincere -

This conversation has to be frank and sincere. You clients need to know that you genuinely are interested in this feedback and want to do whatever you can to please them. Most of all, they need to know that you are not doing this only for your own self-serving needs.

Listen to More than Words - - - - - - - - - -

Gauge their responses. Listen for their hesitations. Watch their facial reactions. Hopefully, you will be able to tell if they are being honest with you.

All this information is useful and vital for crafting your messages and adjusting your marketing plan. It also gives you a sense of how your business is working on a daily basis, where your clients are headed, and what you can do to help them. Take this information back to your marketing plan.

What Happens If They Come?

Be careful what you wish for. You know how you want to improve your business, but you may not be prepared for how it will change your life when it actually happens. You may be inundated with new leads, new clients, and more business than you know what to do with.

A Happy Customer is a Repeat Customer: Why Customer Service is the Key to Success

When clients actually show up to do business with you, your customer service will be more important than ever. This is why you need to make sure you have carefully thought out your plan and have everything in place. You really don't get a second chance to make a first impression. The first time your prospects visit your website or call your office and meet you and your staff in person has a profound impact on the impressions they form.

What Makes You a Happy Customer? - - -

Learn from your own customer service experiences at other businesses. How did the employees make you smile? What did they do to make your experience as positive as possible? Create an internal system that replicates these actions. Your staff needs to know how to efficiently and politely respond to your customers' needs. This goes a long way toward making exceptional customer service a hallmark for your company.

Prepare Your Staff for the Extra Work - - -

Even if you are already known for your customer service, be prepared for the wave of new business that can overwhelm your staff. Remember that you set goals to increase your business, and your staff may not always be able to perform as well under the added pressure. A system will give them the resources they need to respond almost automatically to whatever the customer needs.

Hire Outside Help: The Power of Virtual Marketing Staff - - -

Putting together a marketing plan may seem like a daunting task. It's a lot of work, and it takes time to put it into place. You need help. If you don't have staff on hand, consider hiring a firm like ours to supplement your efforts.

Your virtual marketing staff can help you grow your business by completing different steps so they are done sooner rather than later. It's also cheaper and quicker to outsource this work than it is to go through the hiring process.. Instead of dealing with the paperwork and legal issues that go along with hiring more employees, you can hire our staff on a retainer basis, paying only for the time you use.

We are marketing professionals who can help you design materials, send them to prospects, and take care of regularly scheduled mailings. We're only a phone call away. The cost for this extra assistance is ridiculously low compared to the results you can get, especially when you consider that you don't have to deal with benefits packages, payroll taxes, and staff training.

This improves your company's effectiveness and lets you focus on attending to your clients' needs. As a result, you will be a better executive and will watch your streamlined business use time and resources better.

Putting Everything into Practice

If you've made it this far, I know you have worked your way through this book and are prepared to use direct mail to increase your sales and retain existing customers. To make the implementation a bit easier, I am including a step-by-step guide as well as worksheets to help you pull everything together.

Important

All worksheets and posters can be downloaded, free of charge, at **DirectMailIsNotDead.com**

Reminders

1. **Remember the three ways to grow your business.**

Display the poster in your office, and as ad sales reps visit you to sell their "great advertising bargains," review your marketing plan. Don't spend money on advertising that doesn't help you increase the number of sales, increase the number of customers, or increase the sale price.

2. **Stop focusing on branding.**

Branding is for huge corporations, not for your business. Design your advertising and marketing with a call to action that directs your prospects and clients to a landing page (not just a generic home page). Your contact information—website, phone number, email, etc.—should be on every marketing piece you distribute.

3. **Direct mail is good.**

Utilize well designed postcards, creative sales letters, and trade show mailers to grow your business. Create a system to use drip marketing to existing clients as well as prospects that have shown an interest in your business in the past.

4. **Remember the lifetime value of the customer.**

Calculate the lifetime value of your current customers as well as the lifetime value of your potential customers when you are targeting a new segment in your industry. This will help you know how much you are able to invest in advertising and marketing to obtain these customers. If the lifetime value of your prospect is $5,000, would you spend $50, $100, or more to obtain that client?

5. **Keep in mind the importance of acquisition and retention.**

When planning your marketing campaigns, remember that retention can be more valuable than acquisition. Stay focused on these three ways to grow your business, and remember that 2/3 of the ways involve growing sales from clients you already have!

Three Ways To Grow My Business:

a) Increase the number of our clients.

b) Increase the average size of the sale per client.

c) Increase the number of times our clients return and buy again.

6. **Protect your raving fans.**

Throughout your planning process, remember to keep smothering your current clients with superior service, creating raving fans that will also spread your marketing message. If you are targeting a certain demographic, and your fans are a subset of that demographic, they will talk to others. You want that discussion to be about your firm in a positive manner.

7. **Cultivate a sense of urgency.**

Stacks on your desk are not producing results. Instead, you need a true sense of urgency to get your marketing on track. Set aside time away from the office, if necessary, to get your plans in order. Tell others about your plans so they can help keep you accountable. Set realistic deadlines, and reward yourself as you meet them.

8. **There is no quick fix.**

Remind yourself that marketing is a process, and it will take time to implement and reap the rewards. You already have spent considerable time planning other processes in your business. This is just another one.

9. **People buy from people.**

Your customers are not companies; they are people. Create messages that show how you will help solve problems that people have. When targeting individuals in a firm, picture what that ideal "person" looks like, what their needs are, and why they would purchase from you instead of their current suppliers. The more you have that ideal person in your mind as you craft your message, the more you will be able to talk directly to them.

10. **Create a system.**

Design your marketing plan as a system to keep the plan operating. Assign parts of the plan to people within your organization who will report results to you and keep the plan moving in a forward motion. The better system you create, the better results you will have with less involvement on your part.

11. **Massive action leads to massive results.**

Nothing gets done until you implement your strategies. Massive action requires massive commitment from you and your employees. Everyone needs to know the plan, why you are spending time on your marketing, and what parts they play in growing the business. The more emphasis you place on your plan, the more likely you and your staff will take the steps seriously.

12. **Create a quality USP.**

Creating and integrating your Unique Selling Proposition is critical to your identity. Your USP ties everything together. It tells your staff their mission and lets your clients and prospects know who you are and why they will do business with you. Your USP may evolve over time, but take the time to develop one today.

13. **Use landing pages to gather data about your customers and prospects.**

Your calls to action in your marketing should direct prospects to landing pages instead of your website's home page. Use landing pages as lead generation sources and collect vital information to follow up on through other contact methods.

14. **Use email marketing as part of a comprehensive plan.**

Use email marketing in conjunction with your other marketing efforts, not as the primary advertising media. Marketers have become lazy, thinking that sending emails is effective marketing. The old adage, "you get what you pay for" very much applies to email marketing.

15. **Let your personality shine in your marketing.**

Connect with your clients and prospects by adding some positive personality to your marketing. Attempt to communicate in a way that makes each communication something that they look forward to receiving.

16. **Deadlines are necessary.**

In addition to deadlines for the stages of your marketing plans, you need to have deadlines in your offers. Plan your mailings with enough time to allow clients to meet those deadlines, and create a sense of urgency in them so they respond in a timely manner.

17. **Ask your raving fans for testimonials.**

Your raving fans will be more than happy to provide testimonials to help grow your business. Simply ask them for a short explanation of why they do business with you, and use their testimonials when targeting prospects similar to them. Include their names to create validity and authority.

18. **Get creative with lumpy mail.**

When you send multi-dimensional mail, you pique the recipient's curiosity. Use lumpy mail to tie into the theme of a sales letter or promotion. Be creative and think of new items that you can use, especially items that may be particular to your industry. You can also use fun items that have no relevance to your industry but that your audience can relate to.

19. **Incorporate promotional products in your marketing plan.**

Personalize some of your lumpy mail items by adding your logo and website information. Purchase promotional items that will help you reach your campaign goals and integrate them in your marketing plan. They can do double duty, and you can put them to work at trade shows and in mail campaigns.

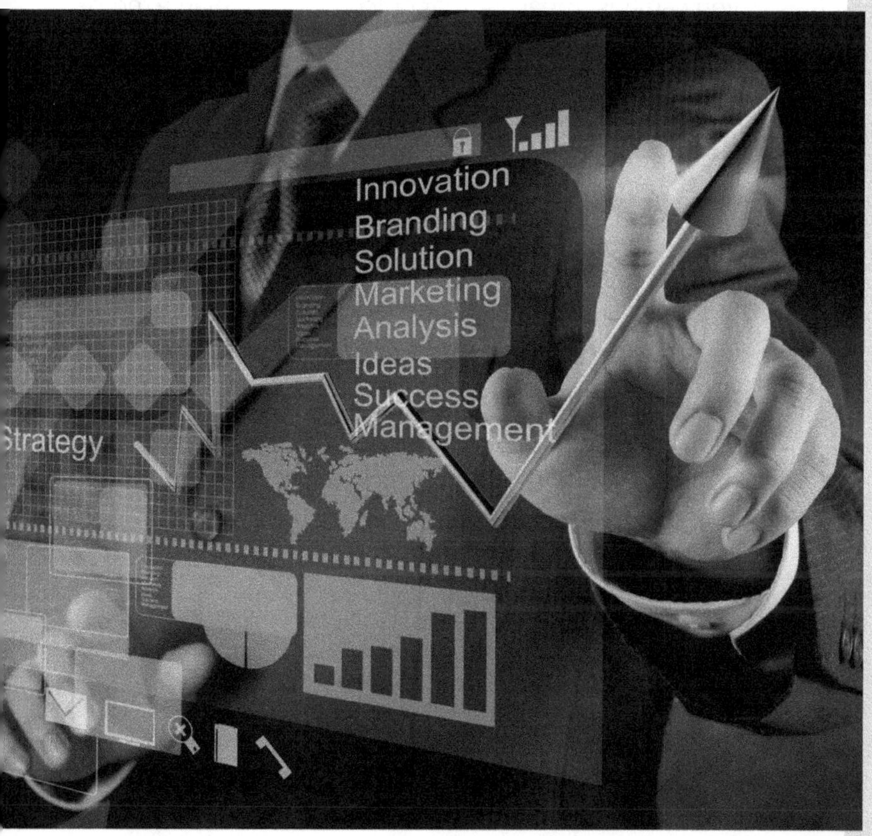

20. Mailing lists are your most important tool.

The success of any mailing campaign depends on a targeted, accurate mailing list. After defining your target prospect, find a reliable, educated source to get you the list you need. Be specific when identifying the information you want, like phone numbers, contact names, or other demographic information, so you don't lose money by asking for additional information after the fact.

21. Metrics help you measure the success of your marketing efforts.

The only way to know if your marketing efforts are working is to measure them. For this you need metrics. Determine the ideal outcome of your mailing and how you can best measure that outcome. Then plan a method to measure those results.

22. What if they come?

Customer service is an essential part of creating your raving fans, so ideally your staff is already trained to provide excellent service. However, sudden increases in inquiries and new clients may cause strains to your internal operations. Be ready and willing to increase the number of employees and train existing staff members to handle these changes. Having a huge influx of new business is great, but not at the expense of losing existing clients in the process.

Visit

www.DirectMailIsNotDead.com/book

As a purchaser of this book you are entitled to a number of free resources to help you implement the many strategies I have given you in the book.

* Poster to remind you:
* **3 Ways To Grow Your Business**
* **Branding Is Not Good** reminder
* Direct Mail samples, in full color
* **Lifetime Value of A Customer** worksheet
* **Unique Selling Proposition** worksheet
* **Headlines That Work** to help craft your offer
* **Marketing Plan** worksheet

www.ingramcontent.com/pod-product-compliance
Lightning Source LLC
Chambersburg PA
CBHW060615210326
41520CB00010B/1352

* 9 7 8 0 6 1 5 9 4 6 2 9 0 *